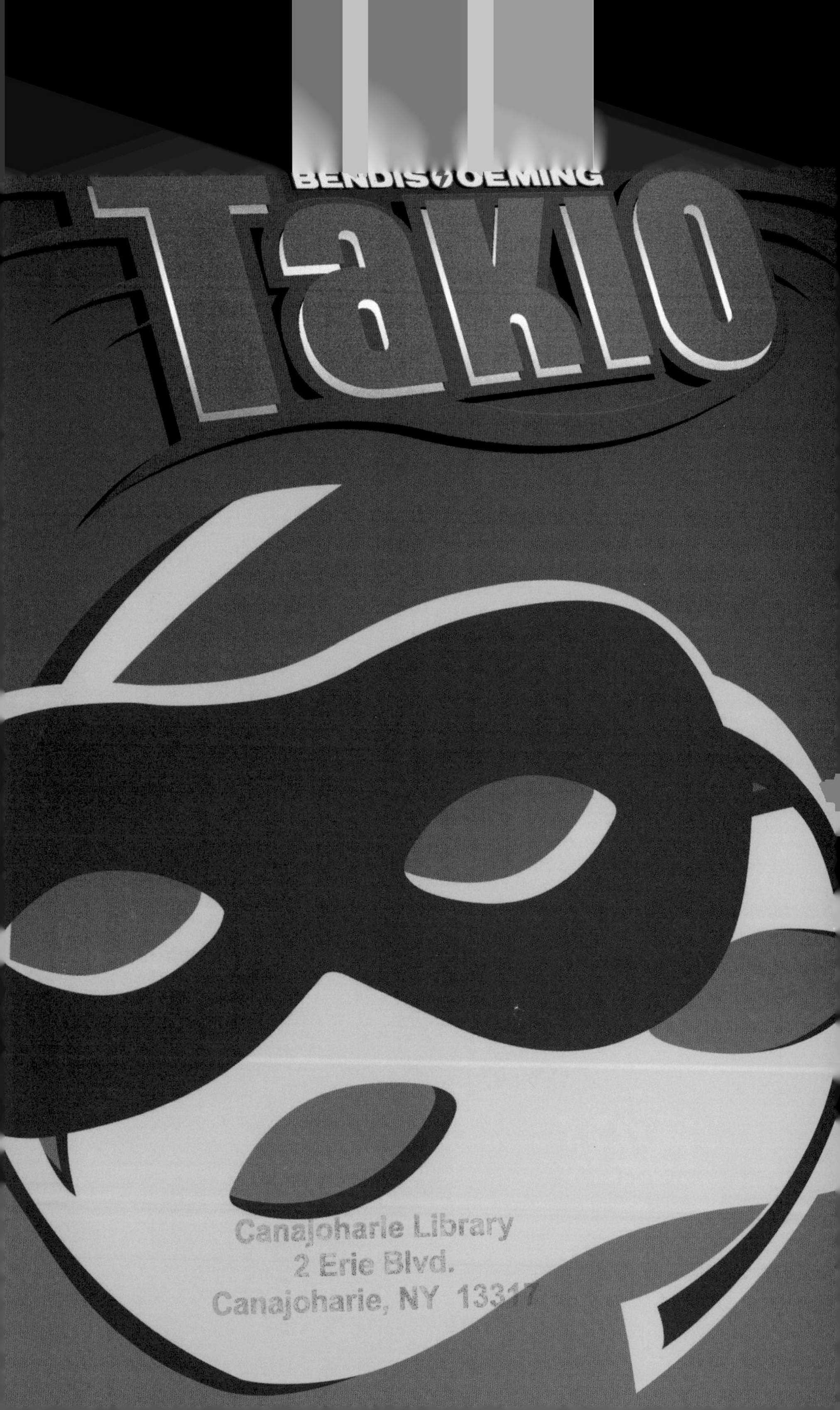
BENDIS/OEMING
TAKIO

BENDIS ◊ OEMING

Takio

CREATED BY
Brian Michael Bendis,
Michael Avon Oeming
& Olivia Bendis

WRITTEN & ILLUSTRATED BY
Brian Michael Bendis
& Michael Avon Oeming

COLORS: Nick Filardi
LETTERS & PRODUCTION: Chris Eliopoulos
EDITOR: Jennifer Grünwald
BOOK DESIGN: Patrick McGrath
COVER DESIGN: Tim Daniel
BUSINESS AFFAIRS: Alisa Bendis

Special thanks to Taki Soma

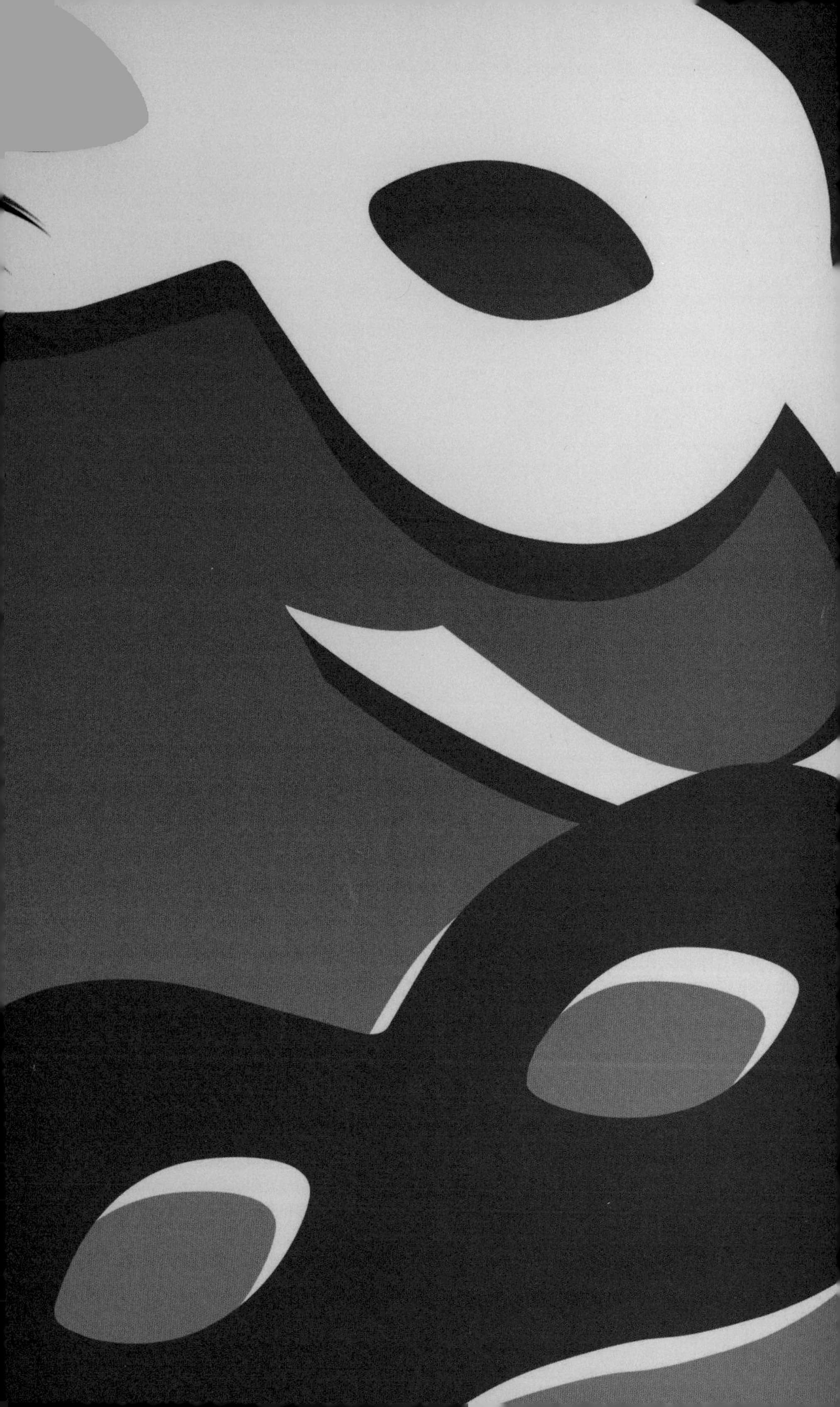

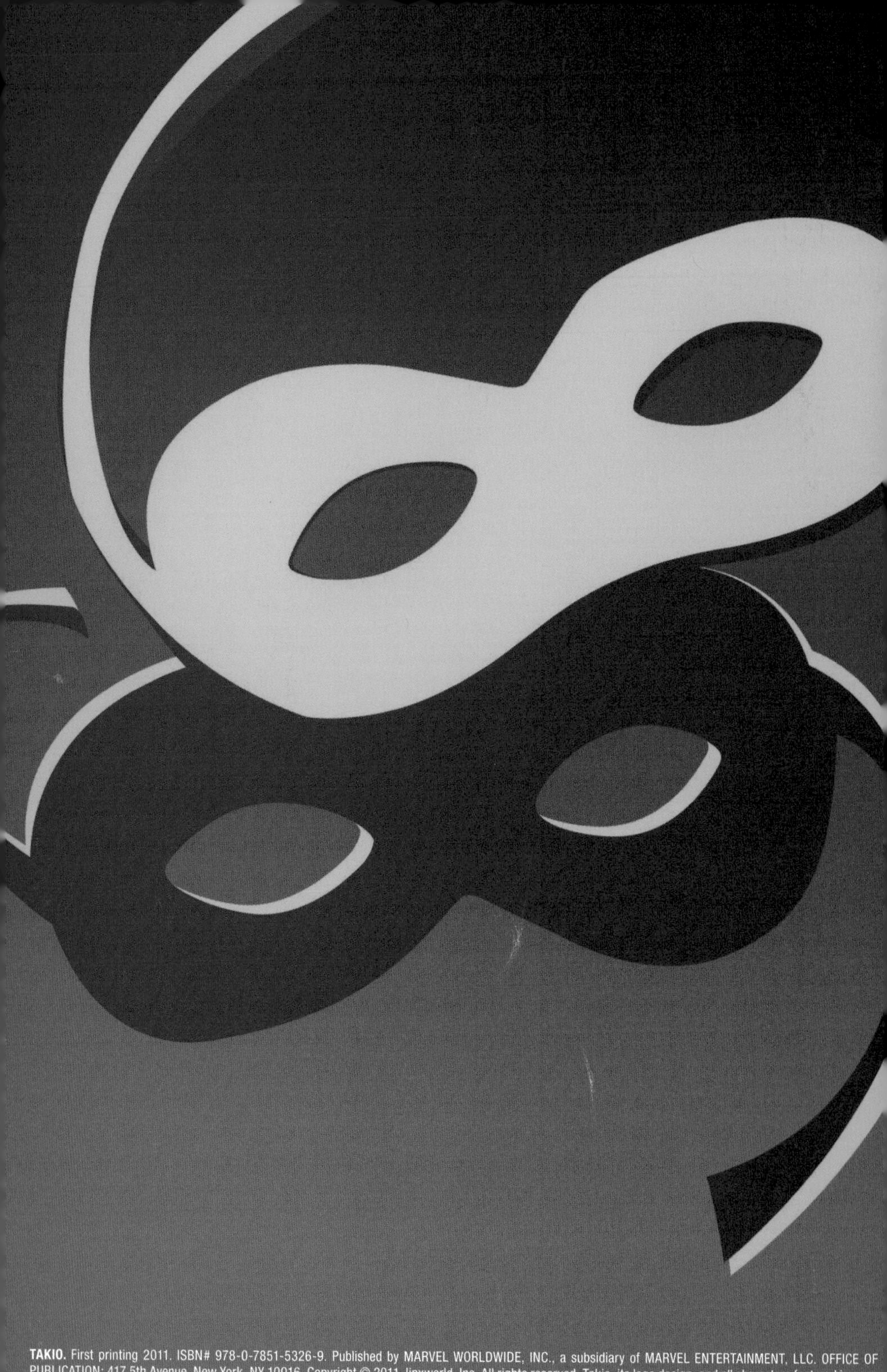

TAKIO. First printing 2011. ISBN# 978-0-7851-5326-9. Published by MARVEL WORLDWIDE, INC., a subsidiary of MARVEL ENTERTAINMENT, LLC. OFFICE OF PUBLICATION: 417 5th Avenue, New York, NY 10016. $9.95 per copy in the U.S. and $11.50 in Canada (GST #R127032852); Canadian Agreement #40668537. **Printed in the U.S.A.**

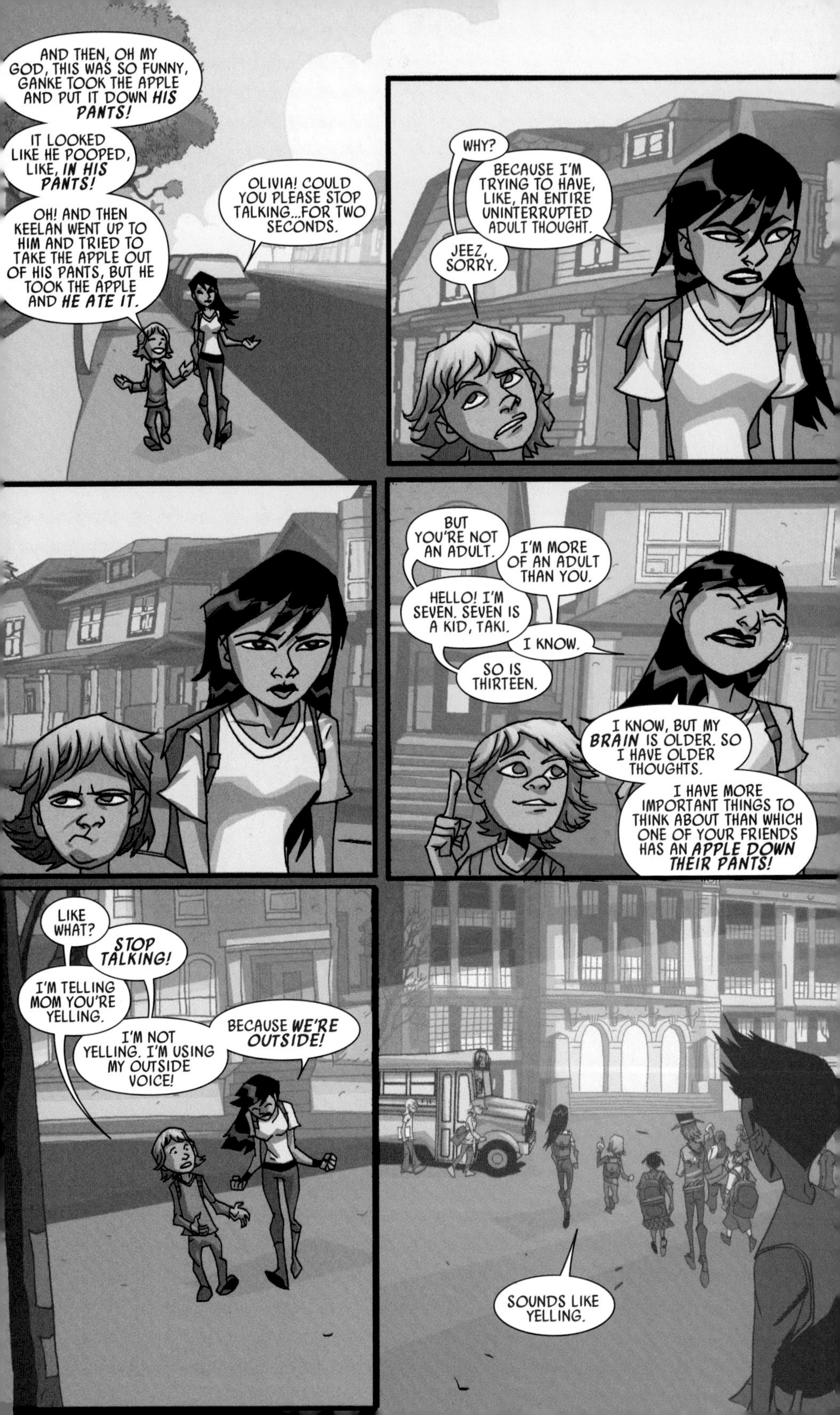

AND THEN, OH MY GOD, THIS WAS SO FUNNY, GANKE TOOK THE APPLE AND PUT IT DOWN *HIS PANTS!*
IT LOOKED LIKE HE POOPED, LIKE, *IN HIS PANTS!*
OH! AND THEN KEELAN WENT UP TO HIM AND TRIED TO TAKE THE APPLE OUT OF HIS PANTS, BUT HE TOOK THE APPLE AND *HE ATE IT.*
OLIVIA! COULD YOU PLEASE STOP TALKING...FOR TWO SECONDS.
WHY?
BECAUSE I'M TRYING TO HAVE, LIKE, AN ENTIRE UNINTERRUPTED ADULT THOUGHT.
JEEZ, SORRY.
BUT YOU'RE NOT AN ADULT.
I'M MORE OF AN ADULT THAN YOU.
HELLO! I'M SEVEN. SEVEN IS A KID, TAKI.
I KNOW.
SO IS THIRTEEN.
I KNOW, BUT MY *BRAIN* IS OLDER. SO I HAVE OLDER THOUGHTS.
I HAVE MORE IMPORTANT THINGS TO THINK ABOUT THAN WHICH ONE OF YOUR FRIENDS HAS AN *APPLE DOWN THEIR PANTS!*
LIKE WHAT?
STOP TALKING!
I'M TELLING MOM YOU'RE YELLING.
I'M NOT YELLING. I'M USING MY OUTSIDE VOICE!
BECAUSE *WE'RE OUTSIDE!*
SOUNDS LIKE YELLING.

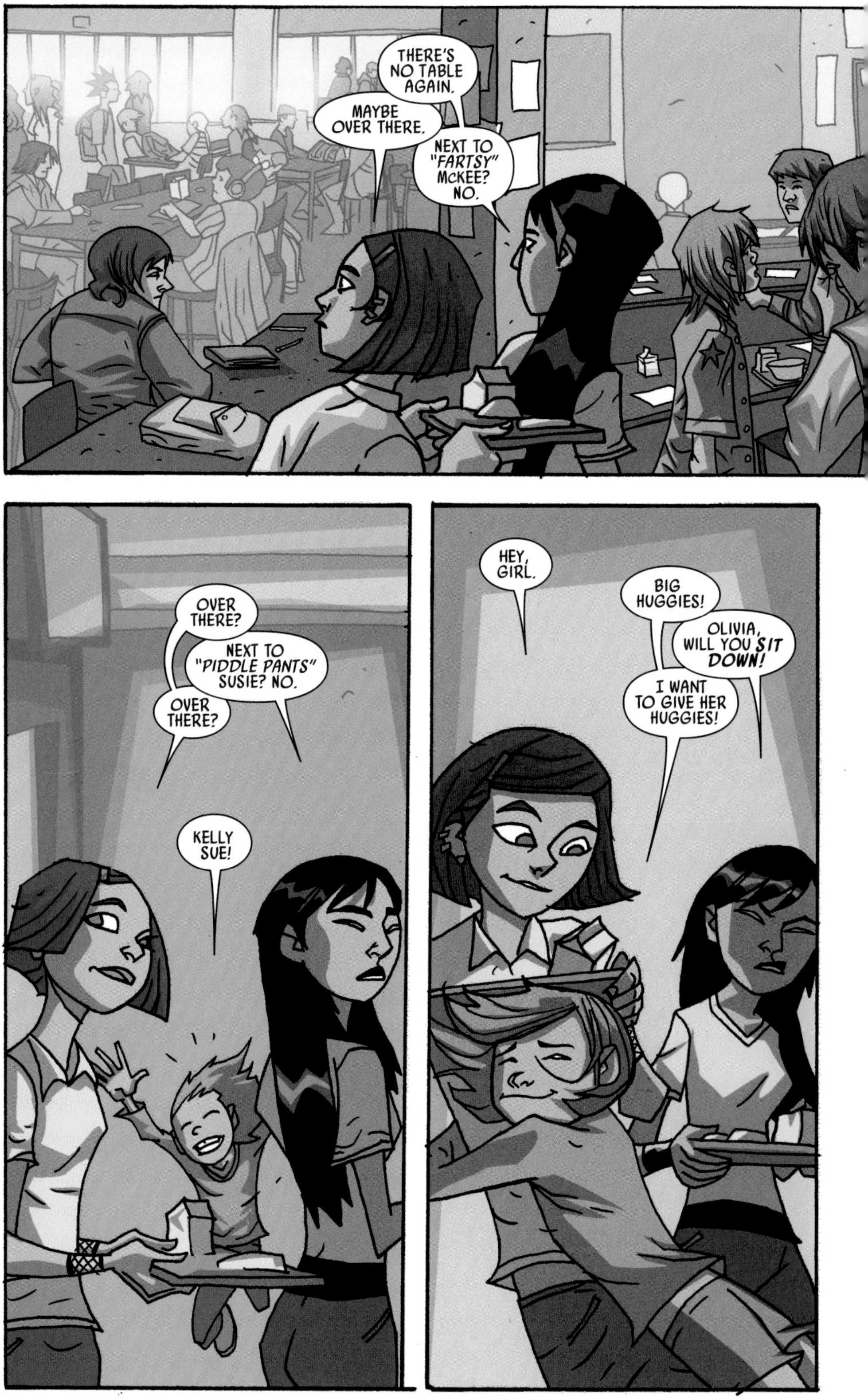
MAYBE OVER THERE.
THERE'S NO TABLE AGAIN.
NEXT TO "FARTSY" McKEE? NO.
OVER THERE?
NEXT TO "PIDDLE PANTS" SUSIE? NO.
OVER THERE?
KELLY SUE!
HEY, GIRL.
BIG HUGGIES!
OLIVIA, WILL YOU SIT DOWN!
I WANT TO GIVE HER HUGGIES!

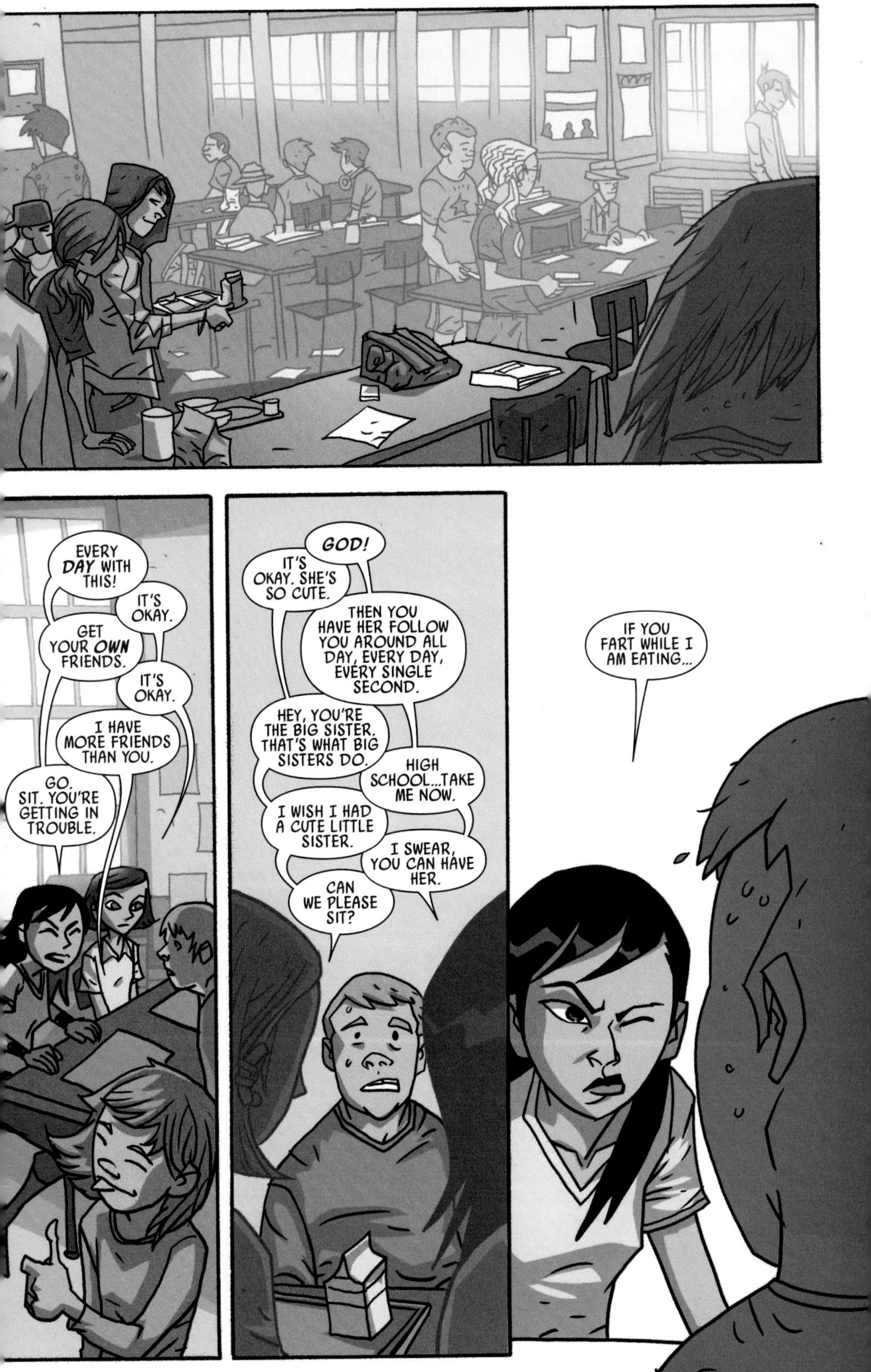
EVERY DAY WITH THIS!
IT'S OKAY.
GET YOUR OWN FRIENDS.
IT'S OKAY.
I HAVE MORE FRIENDS THAN YOU.
GO. SIT. YOU'RE GETTING IN TROUBLE.
GOD!
IT'S OKAY. SHE'S SO CUTE.
THEN YOU HAVE HER FOLLOW YOU AROUND ALL DAY, EVERY DAY, EVERY SINGLE SECOND.
HEY, YOU'RE THE BIG SISTER. THAT'S WHAT BIG SISTERS DO.
HIGH SCHOOL...TAKE ME NOW.
I WISH I HAD A CUTE LITTLE SISTER.
I SWEAR, YOU CAN HAVE HER.
CAN WE PLEASE SIT?
IF YOU FART WHILE I AM EATING...

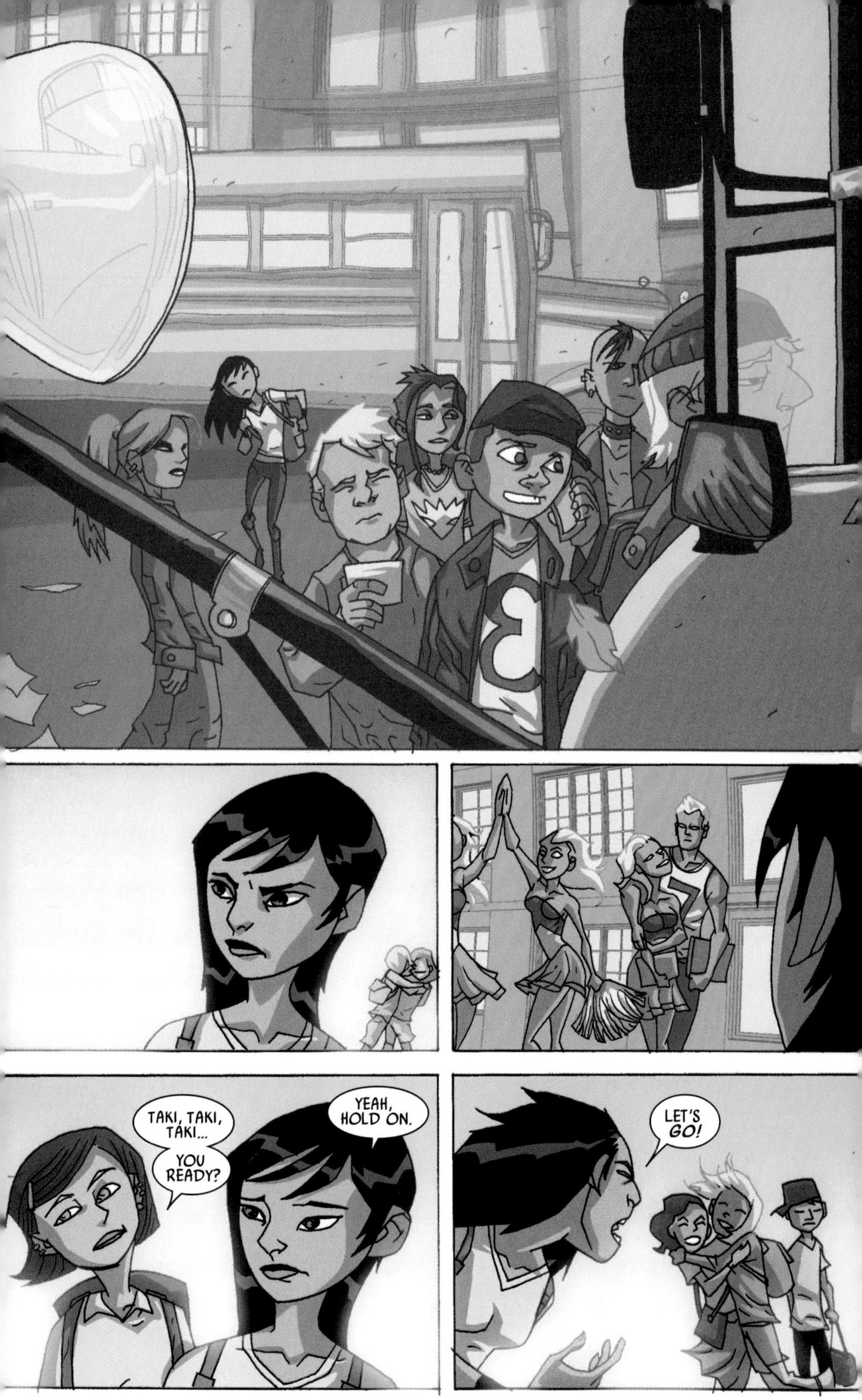
TAKI, TAKI, TAKI...
YOU READY?
YEAH, HOLD ON.
LET'S GO!

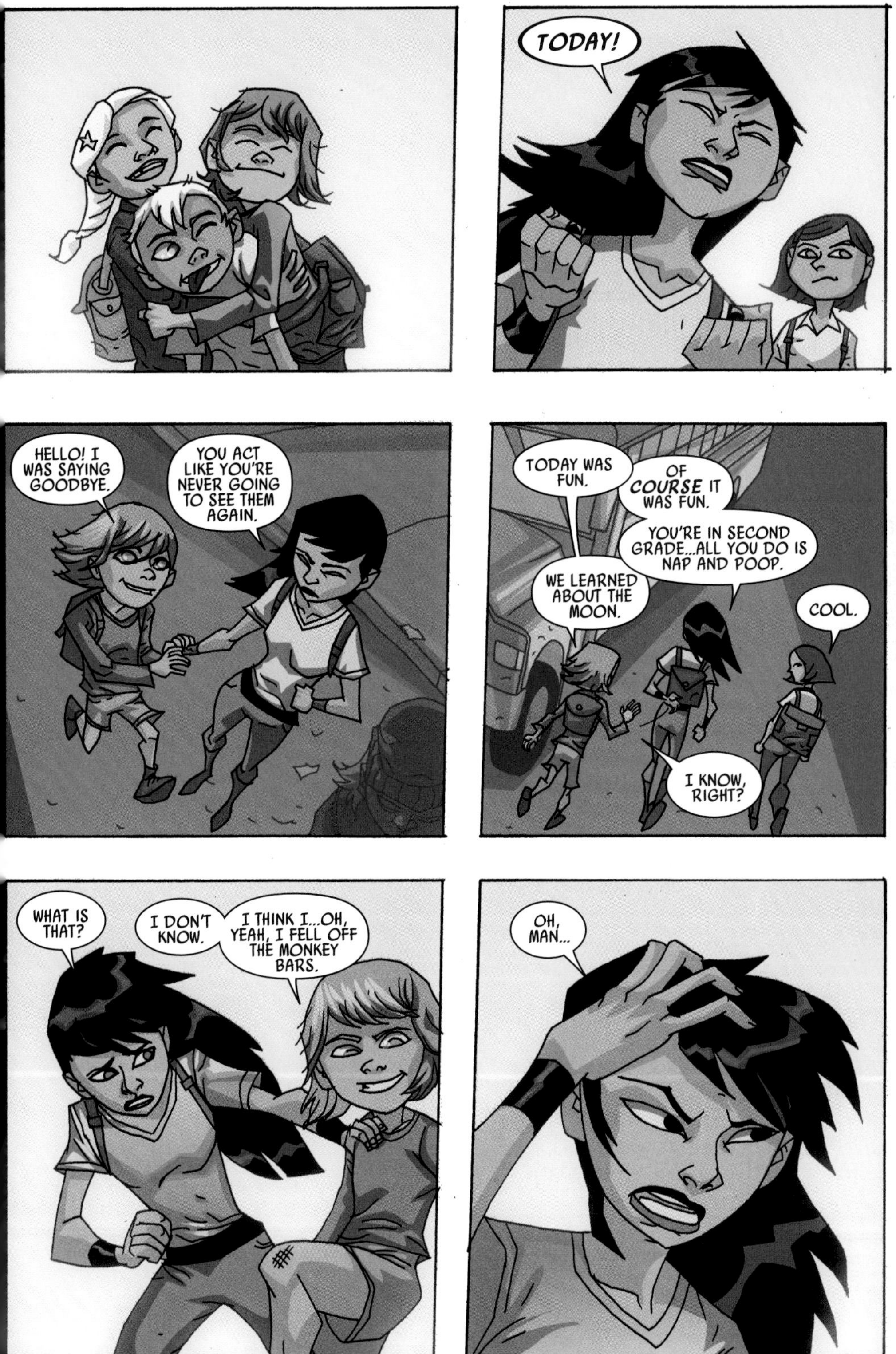
TODAY!
HELLO! I WAS SAYING GOODBYE.
YOU ACT LIKE YOU'RE NEVER GOING TO SEE THEM AGAIN.
TODAY WAS FUN.
OF COURSE IT WAS FUN.
YOU'RE IN SECOND GRADE...ALL YOU DO IS NAP AND POOP.
WE LEARNED ABOUT THE MOON.
COOL.
I KNOW, RIGHT?
WHAT IS THAT?
I DON'T KNOW.
I THINK I...OH, YEAH, I FELL OFF THE MONKEY BARS.
OH, MAN...

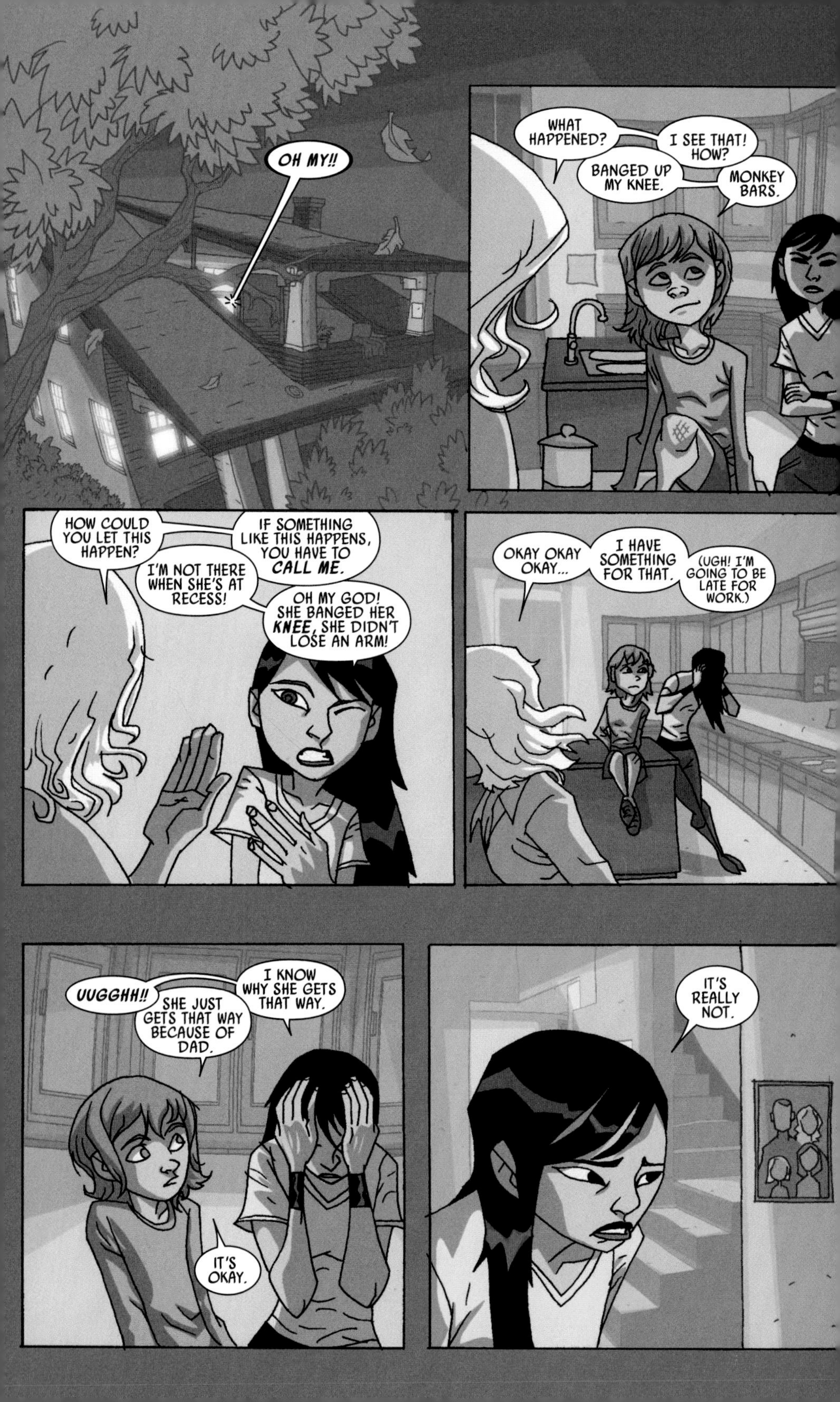
OH MY!!
WHAT HAPPENED?
I SEE THAT! HOW?
BANGED UP MY KNEE.
MONKEY BARS.
HOW COULD YOU LET THIS HAPPEN?
IF SOMETHING LIKE THIS HAPPENS, YOU HAVE TO CALL ME.
I'M NOT THERE WHEN SHE'S AT RECESS!
OH MY GOD! SHE BANGED HER KNEE, SHE DIDN'T LOSE AN ARM!
OKAY OKAY OKAY...
I HAVE SOMETHING FOR THAT.
(UGH! I'M GOING TO BE LATE FOR WORK.)
UUGGHH!!
I KNOW WHY SHE GETS THAT WAY.
SHE JUST GETS THAT WAY BECAUSE OF DAD.
IT'S OKAY.
IT'S REALLY NOT.

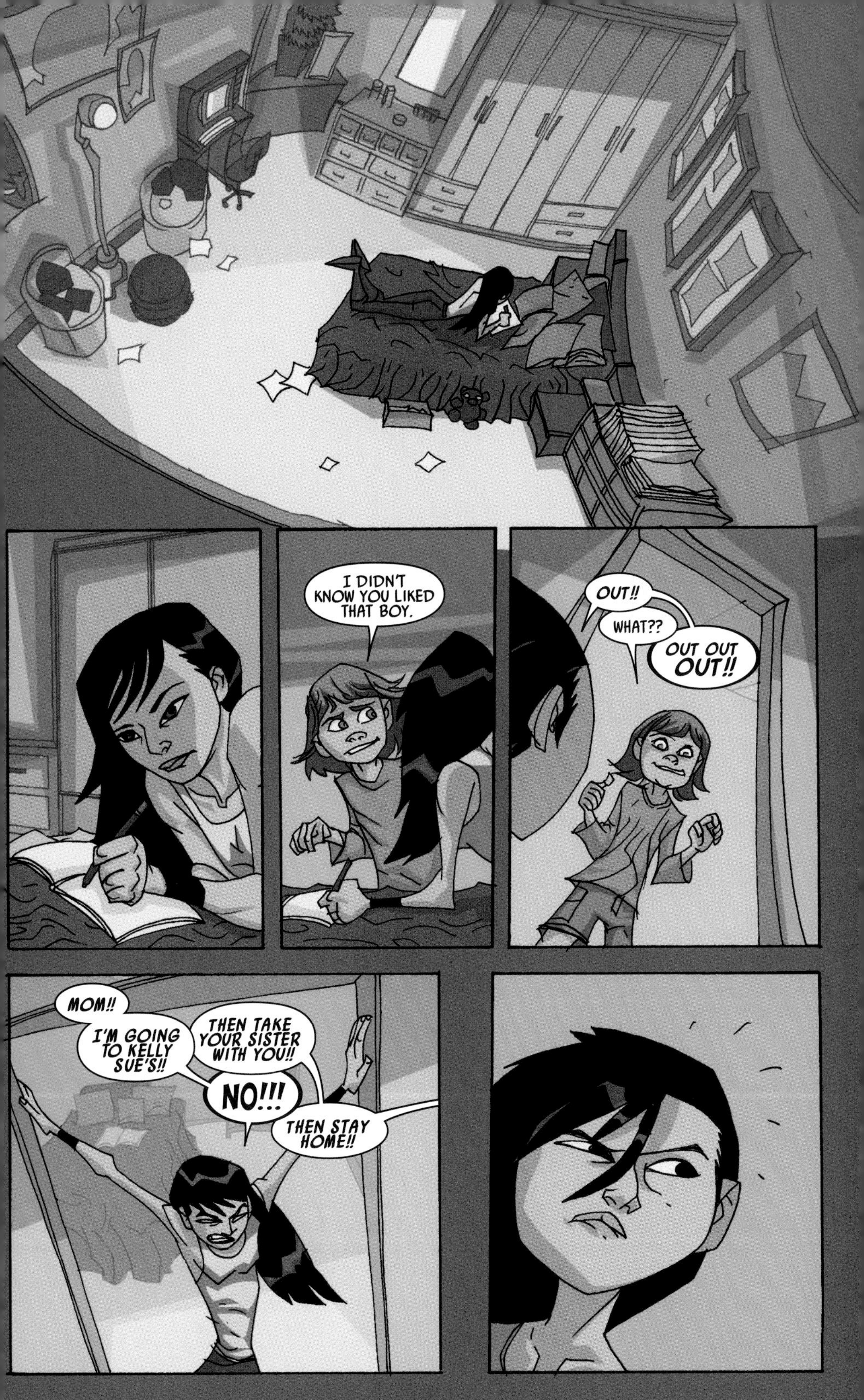
I DIDN'T KNOW YOU LIKED THAT BOY.
OUT!!
WHAT??
OUT OUT OUT!!
MOM!!
I'M GOING TO KELLY SUE'S!!
THEN TAKE YOUR SISTER WITH YOU!!
NO!!!
THEN STAY HOME!!

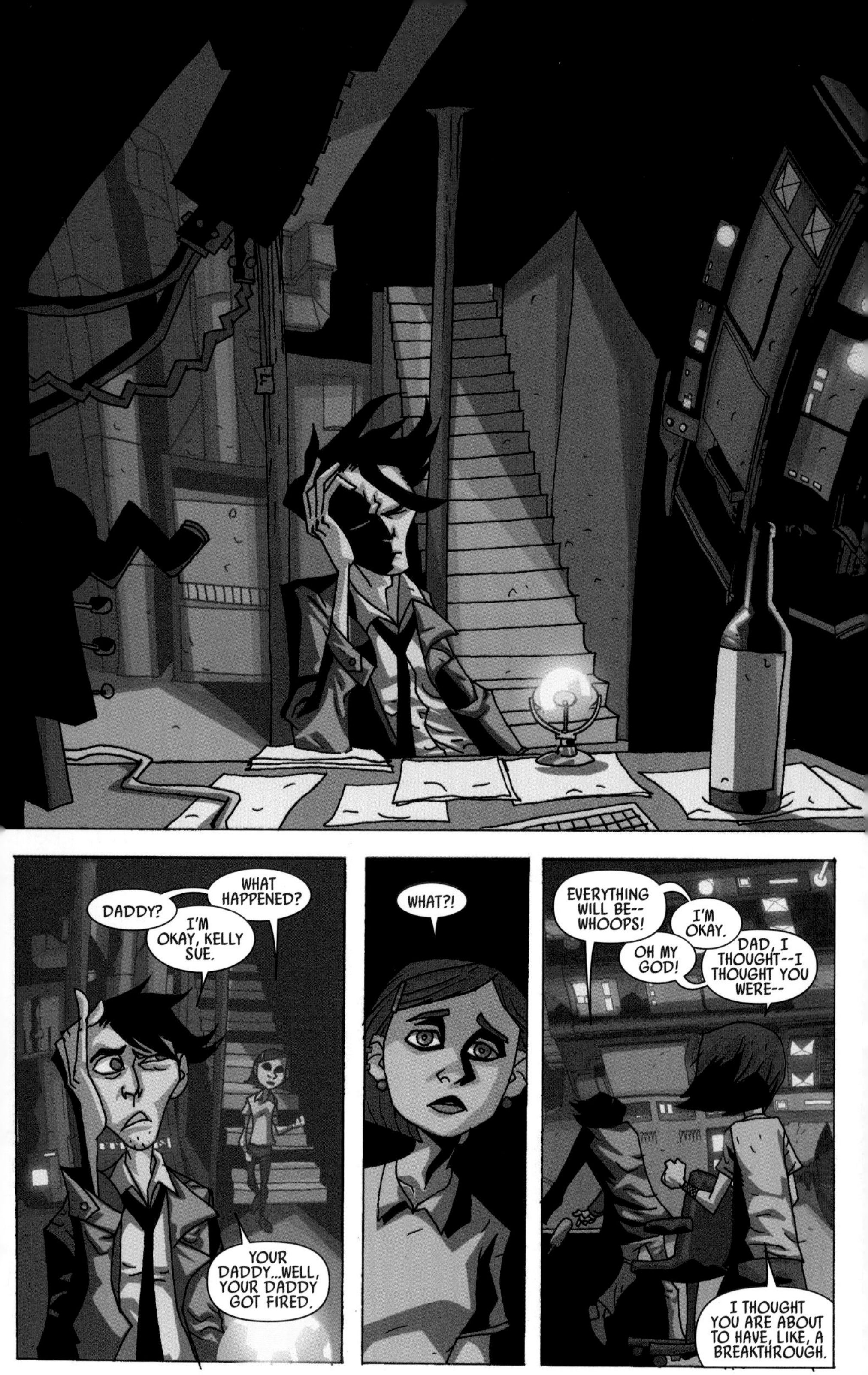
DADDY?
WHAT HAPPENED?
I'M OKAY, KELLY SUE.
YOUR DADDY...WELL, YOUR DADDY GOT FIRED.
WHAT?!
EVERYTHING WILL BE--WHOOPS!
I'M OKAY.
OH MY GOD!
DAD, I THOUGHT--I THOUGHT YOU WERE--
I THOUGHT YOU ARE ABOUT TO HAVE, LIKE, A BREAKTHROUGH.

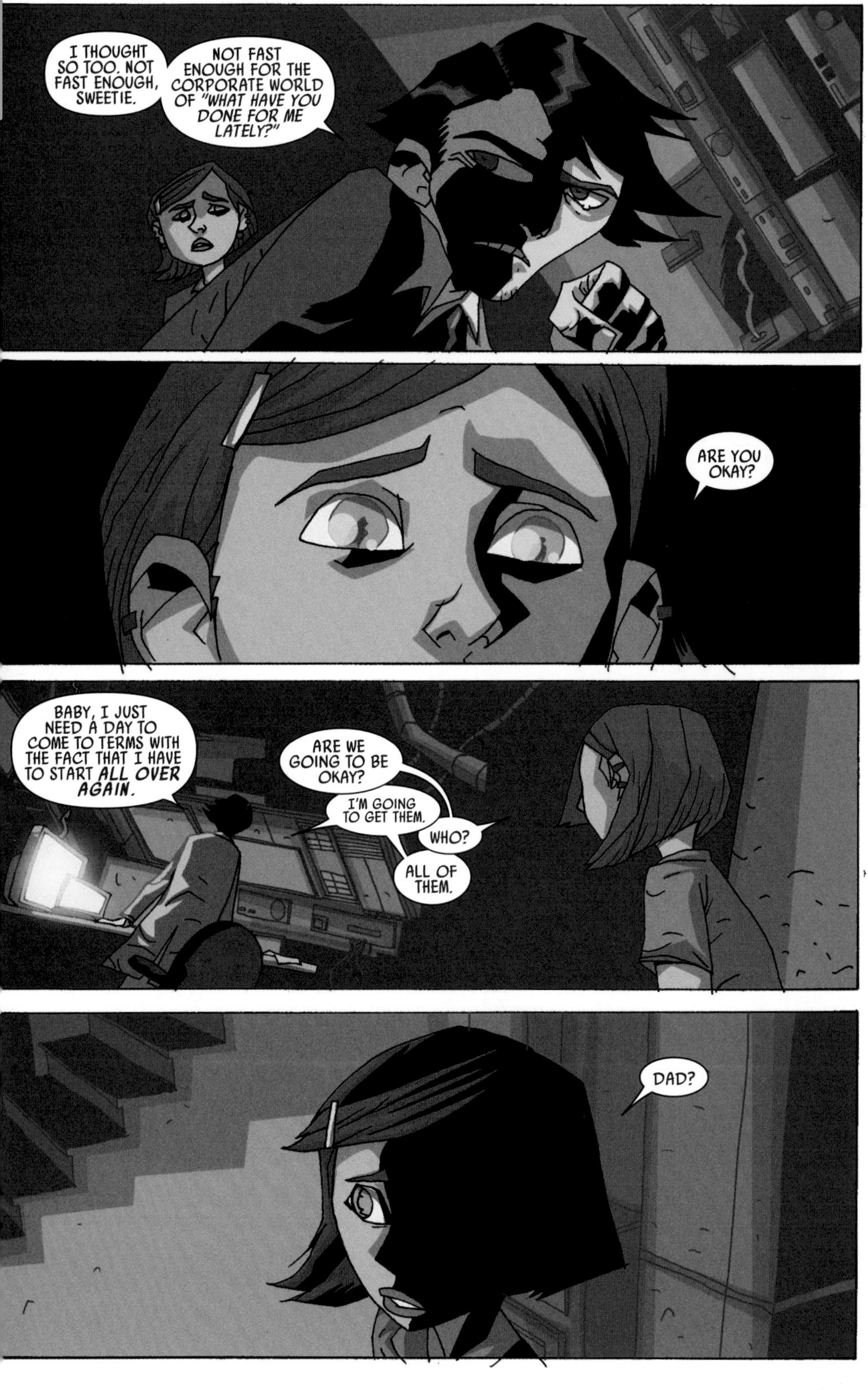
I THOUGHT SO TOO. NOT FAST ENOUGH, SWEETIE.
NOT FAST ENOUGH FOR THE CORPORATE WORLD OF "WHAT HAVE YOU DONE FOR ME LATELY?"
ARE YOU OKAY?
BABY, I JUST NEED A DAY TO COME TO TERMS WITH THE FACT THAT I HAVE TO START ALL OVER AGAIN.
ARE WE GOING TO BE OKAY?
I'M GOING TO GET THEM.
WHO?
ALL OF THEM.
DAD?

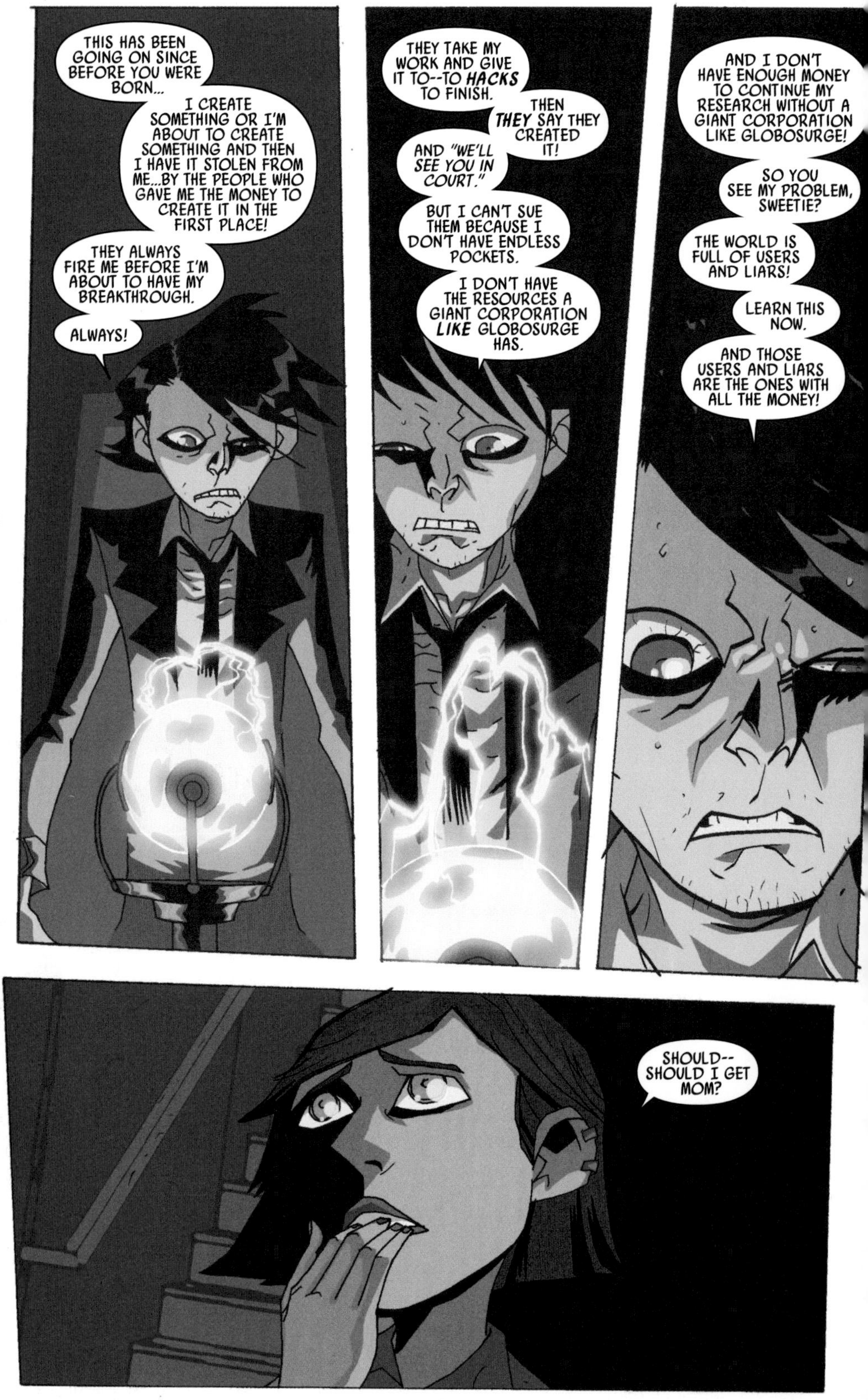

THIS HAS BEEN GOING ON SINCE BEFORE YOU WERE BORN...
I CREATE SOMETHING OR I'M ABOUT TO CREATE SOMETHING AND THEN I HAVE IT STOLEN FROM ME...BY THE PEOPLE WHO GAVE ME THE MONEY TO CREATE IT IN THE FIRST PLACE!
THEY ALWAYS FIRE ME BEFORE I'M ABOUT TO HAVE MY BREAKTHROUGH.
ALWAYS!
THEY TAKE MY WORK AND GIVE IT TO--TO HACKS TO FINISH.
THEN THEY SAY THEY CREATED IT!
AND "WE'LL SEE YOU IN COURT."
BUT I CAN'T SUE THEM BECAUSE I DON'T HAVE ENDLESS POCKETS.
I DON'T HAVE THE RESOURCES A GIANT CORPORATION LIKE GLOBOSURGE HAS.
AND I DON'T HAVE ENOUGH MONEY TO CONTINUE MY RESEARCH WITHOUT A GIANT CORPORATION LIKE GLOBOSURGE!
SO YOU SEE MY PROBLEM, SWEETIE?
THE WORLD IS FULL OF USERS AND LIARS!
LEARN THIS NOW.
AND THOSE USERS AND LIARS ARE THE ONES WITH ALL THE MONEY!
SHOULD-- SHOULD I GET MOM?

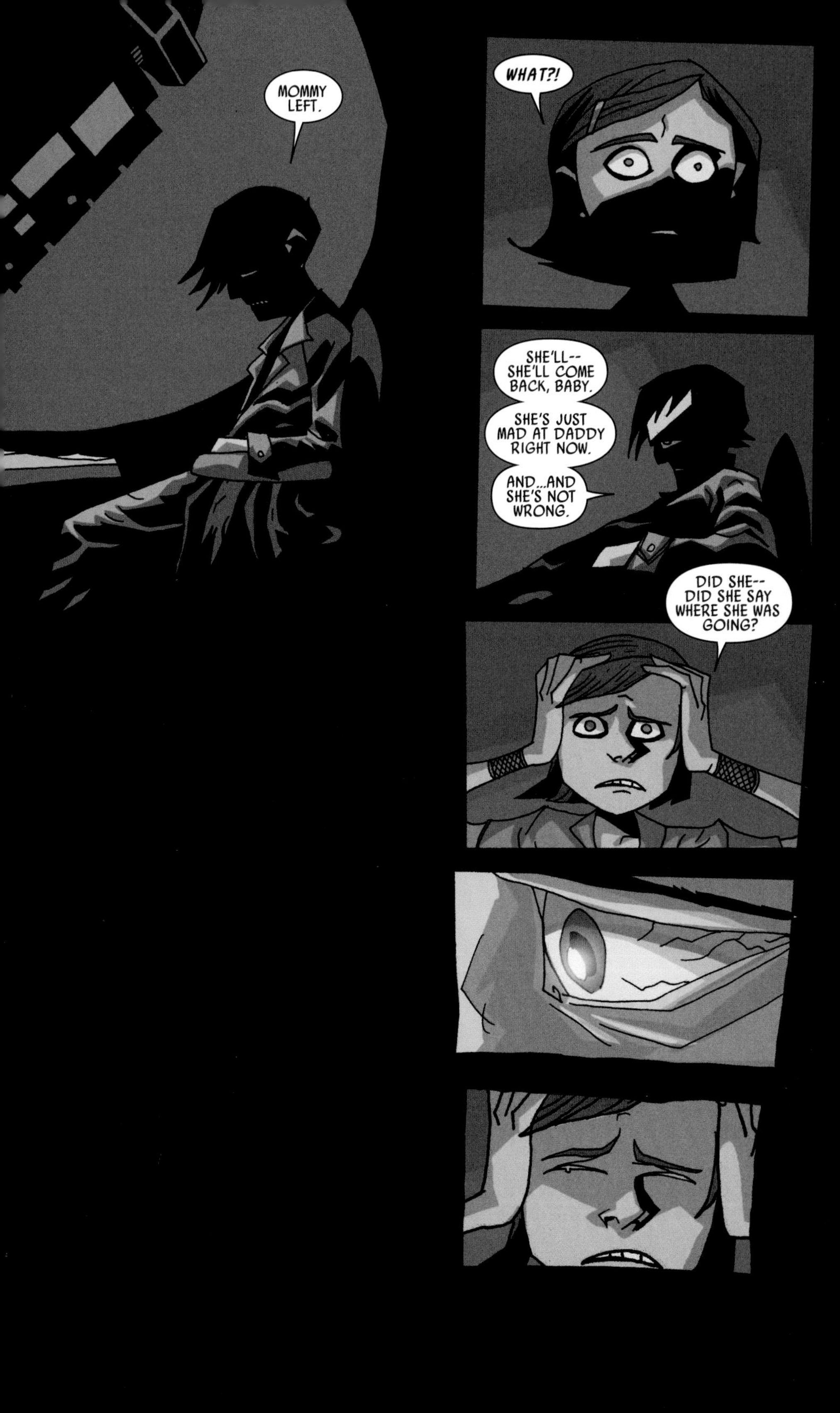
MOMMY LEFT.
WHAT?!
SHE'LL-- SHE'LL COME BACK, BABY.
SHE'S JUST MAD AT DADDY RIGHT NOW.
AND...AND SHE'S NOT WRONG.
DID SHE-- DID SHE SAY WHERE SHE WAS GOING?

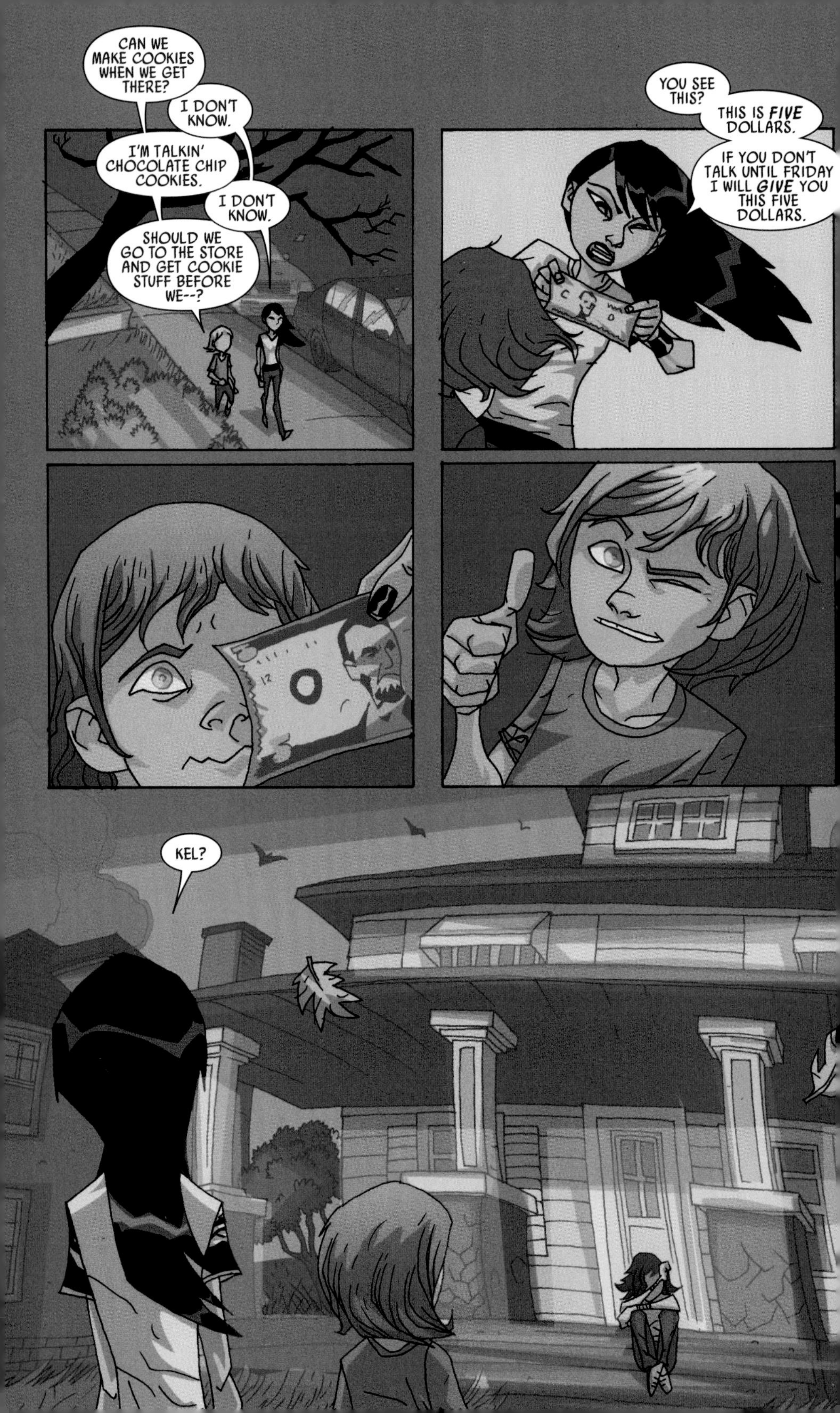
CAN WE MAKE COOKIES WHEN WE GET THERE?
I DON'T KNOW.
I'M TALKIN' CHOCOLATE CHIP COOKIES.
I DON'T KNOW.
SHOULD WE GO TO THE STORE AND GET COOKIE STUFF BEFORE WE--?
YOU SEE THIS?
THIS IS FIVE DOLLARS.
IF YOU DON'T TALK UNTIL FRIDAY I WILL GIVE YOU THIS FIVE DOLLARS.
KEL?

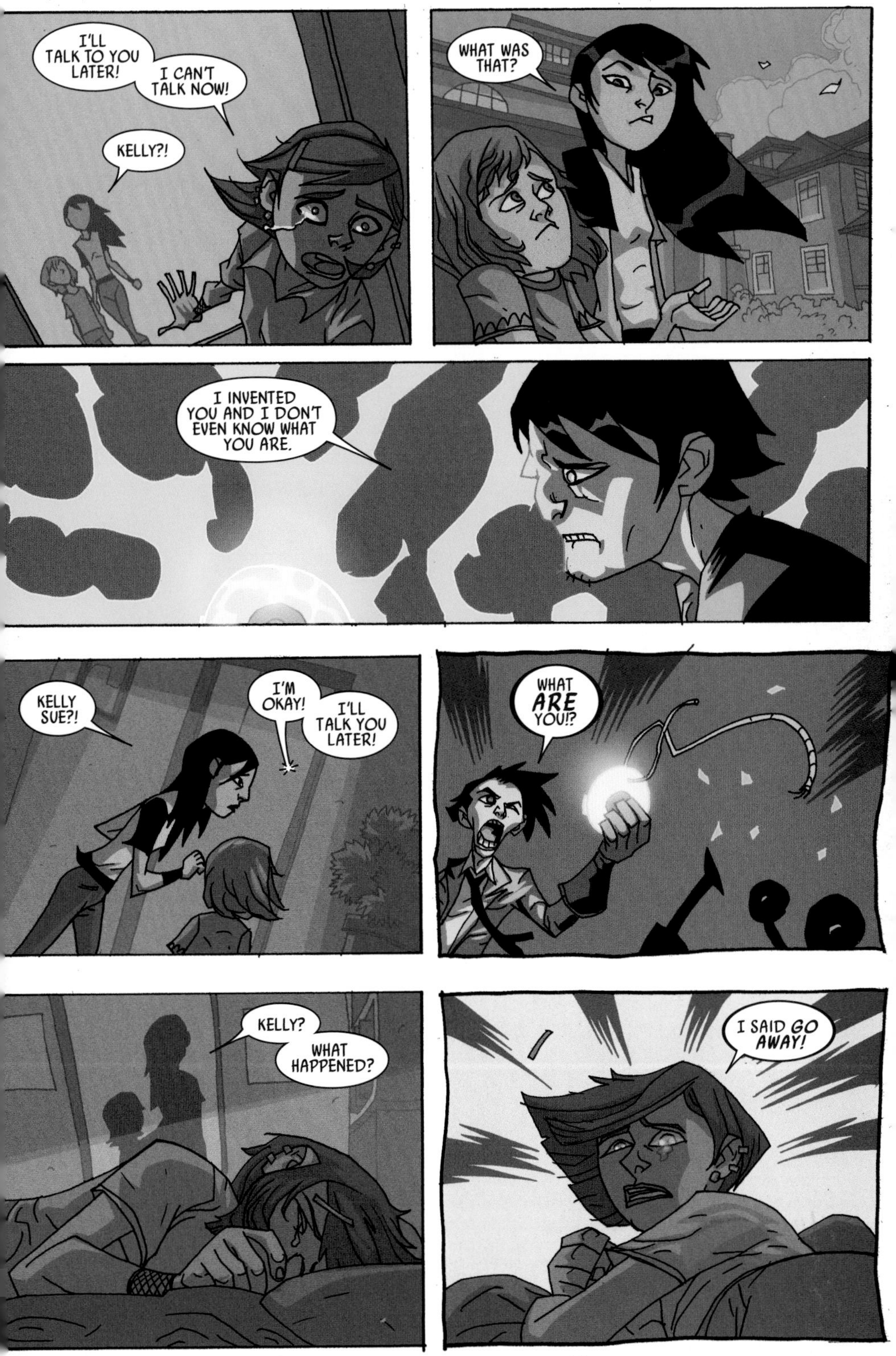
I'LL TALK TO YOU LATER!
I CAN'T TALK NOW!
KELLY?!
WHAT WAS THAT?
I INVENTED YOU AND I DON'T EVEN KNOW WHAT YOU ARE.
KELLY SUE?!
I'M OKAY!
I'LL TALK YOU LATER!
WHAT ARE YOU!?
KELLY?
WHAT HAPPENED?
I SAID GO AWAY!

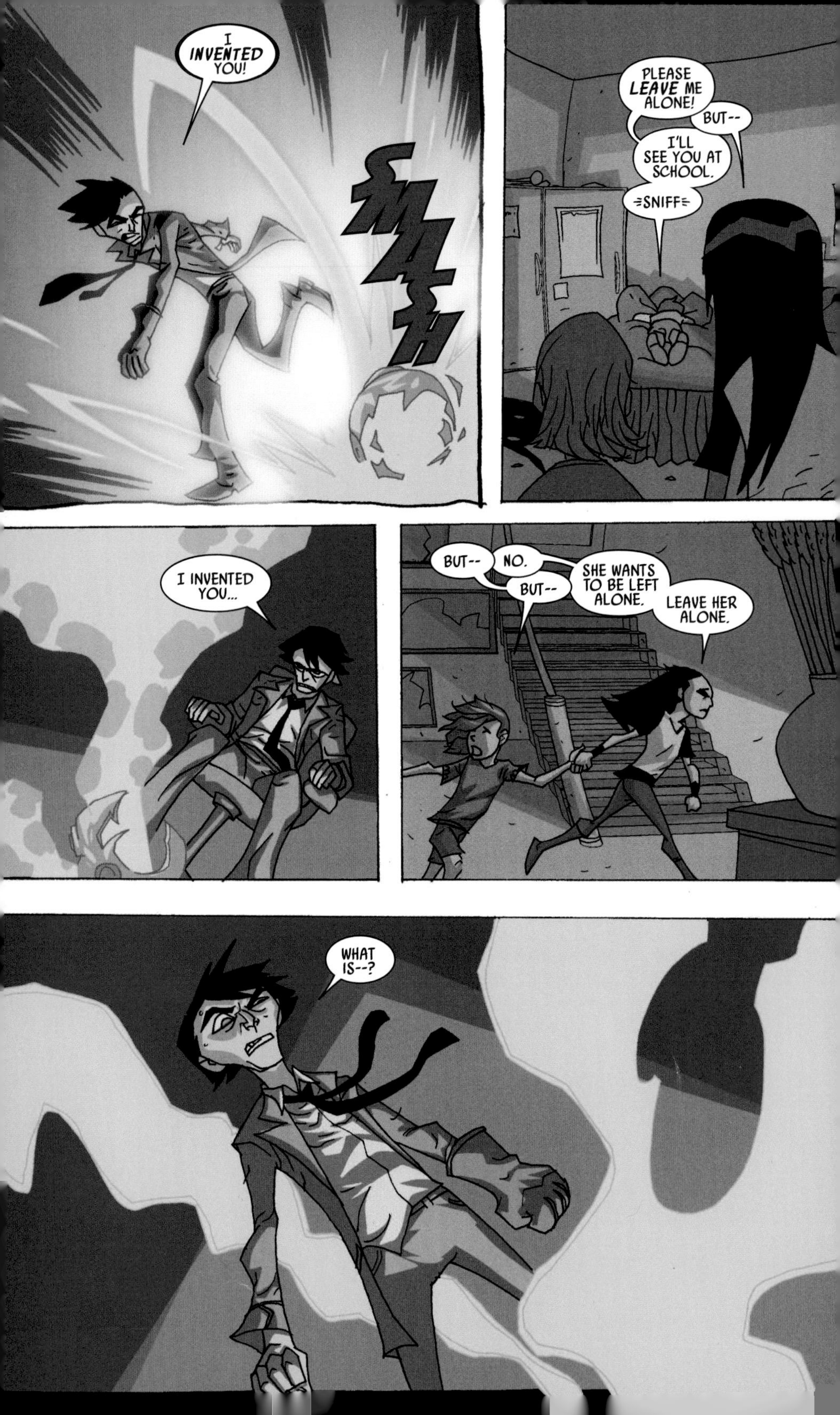
I INVENTED YOU!
SMASH
PLEASE LEAVE ME ALONE!
BUT--
I'LL SEE YOU AT SCHOOL.
=SNIFF=
I INVENTED YOU...
BUT--
NO.
BUT--
SHE WANTS TO BE LEFT ALONE.
LEAVE HER ALONE.
WHAT IS--?

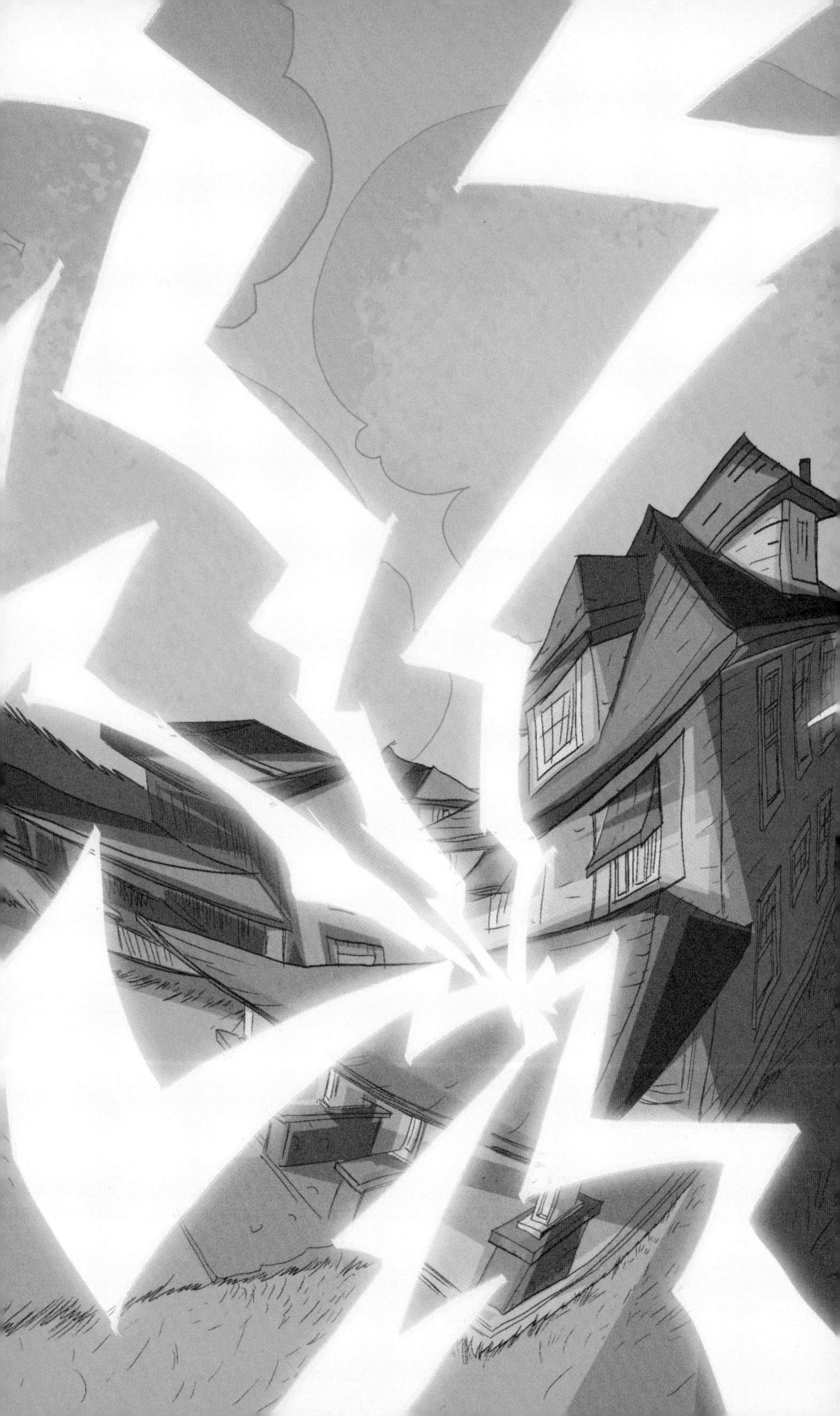

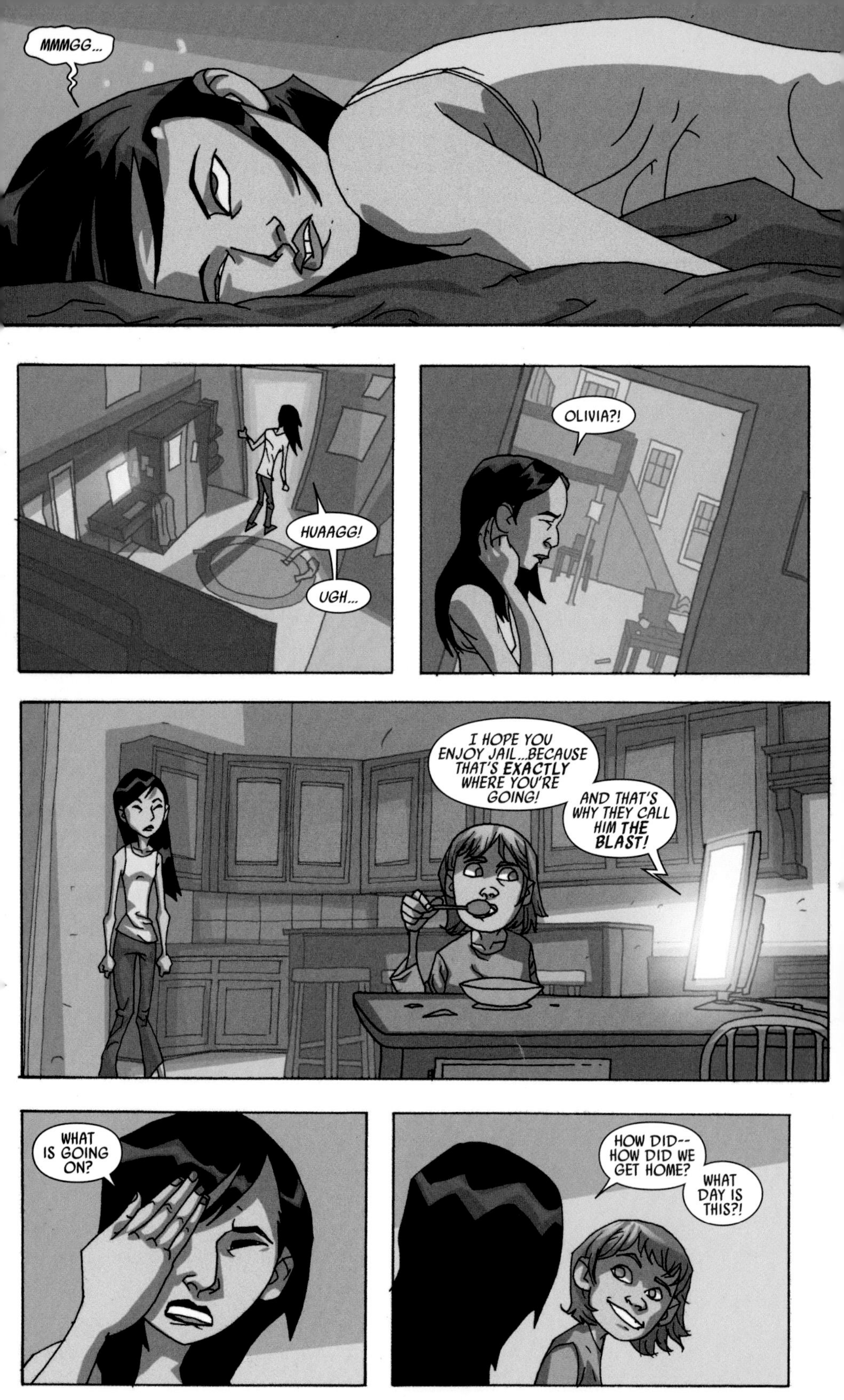
MMMGG...
HUAAGG!
UGH...
OLIVIA?!
I HOPE YOU ENJOY JAIL...BECAUSE THAT'S EXACTLY WHERE YOU'RE GOING!
AND THAT'S WHY THEY CALL HIM THE BLAST!
WHAT IS GOING ON?
HOW DID-- HOW DID WE GET HOME?
WHAT DAY IS THIS?!

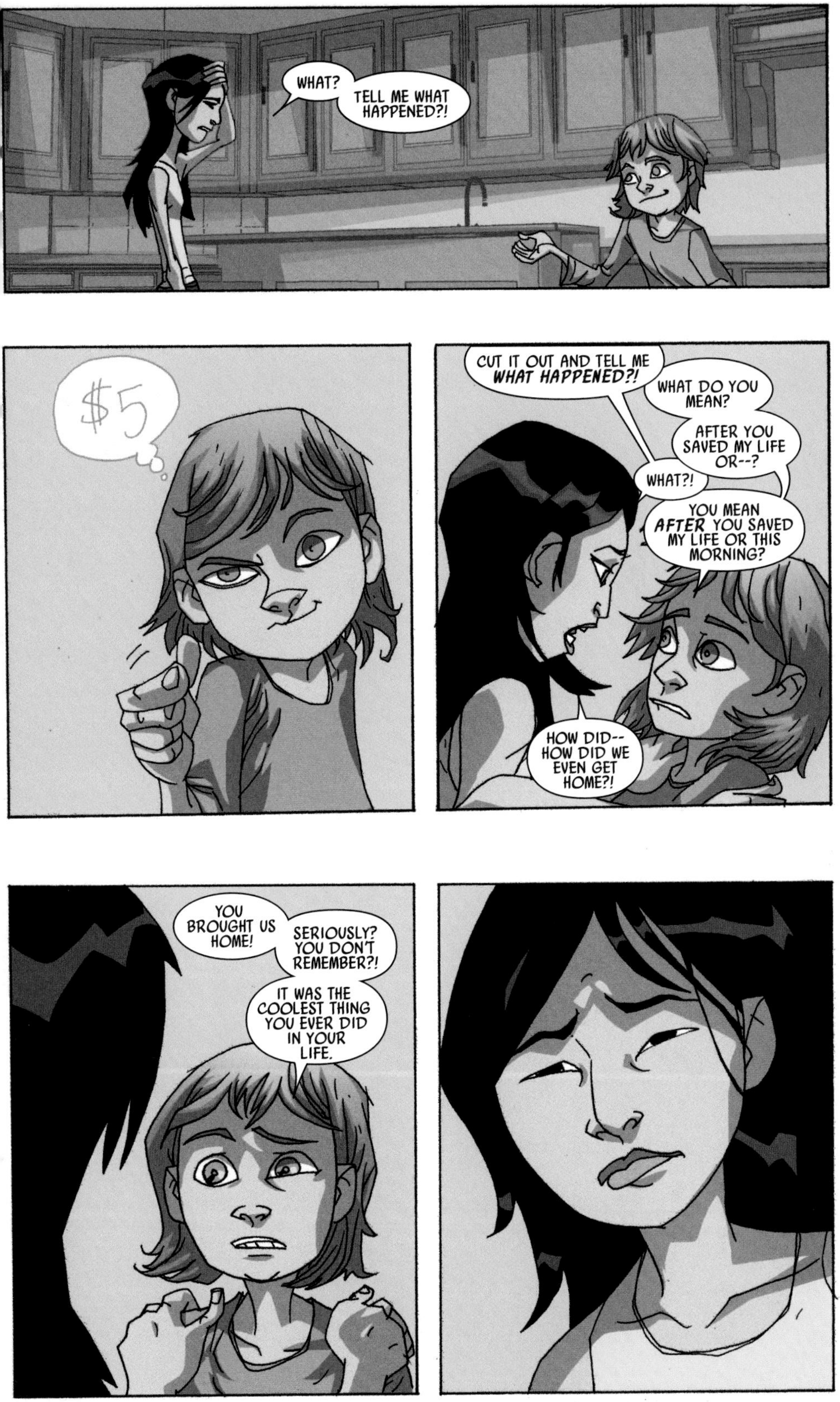

WHAT?
TELL ME WHAT HAPPENED?!
$5
CUT IT OUT AND TELL ME WHAT HAPPENED?!
WHAT DO YOU MEAN?
AFTER YOU SAVED MY LIFE OR--?
WHAT?!
YOU MEAN AFTER YOU SAVED MY LIFE OR THIS MORNING?
HOW DID-- HOW DID WE EVEN GET HOME?!
YOU BROUGHT US HOME!
SERIOUSLY? YOU DON'T REMEMBER?!
IT WAS THE COOLEST THING YOU EVER DID IN YOUR LIFE.

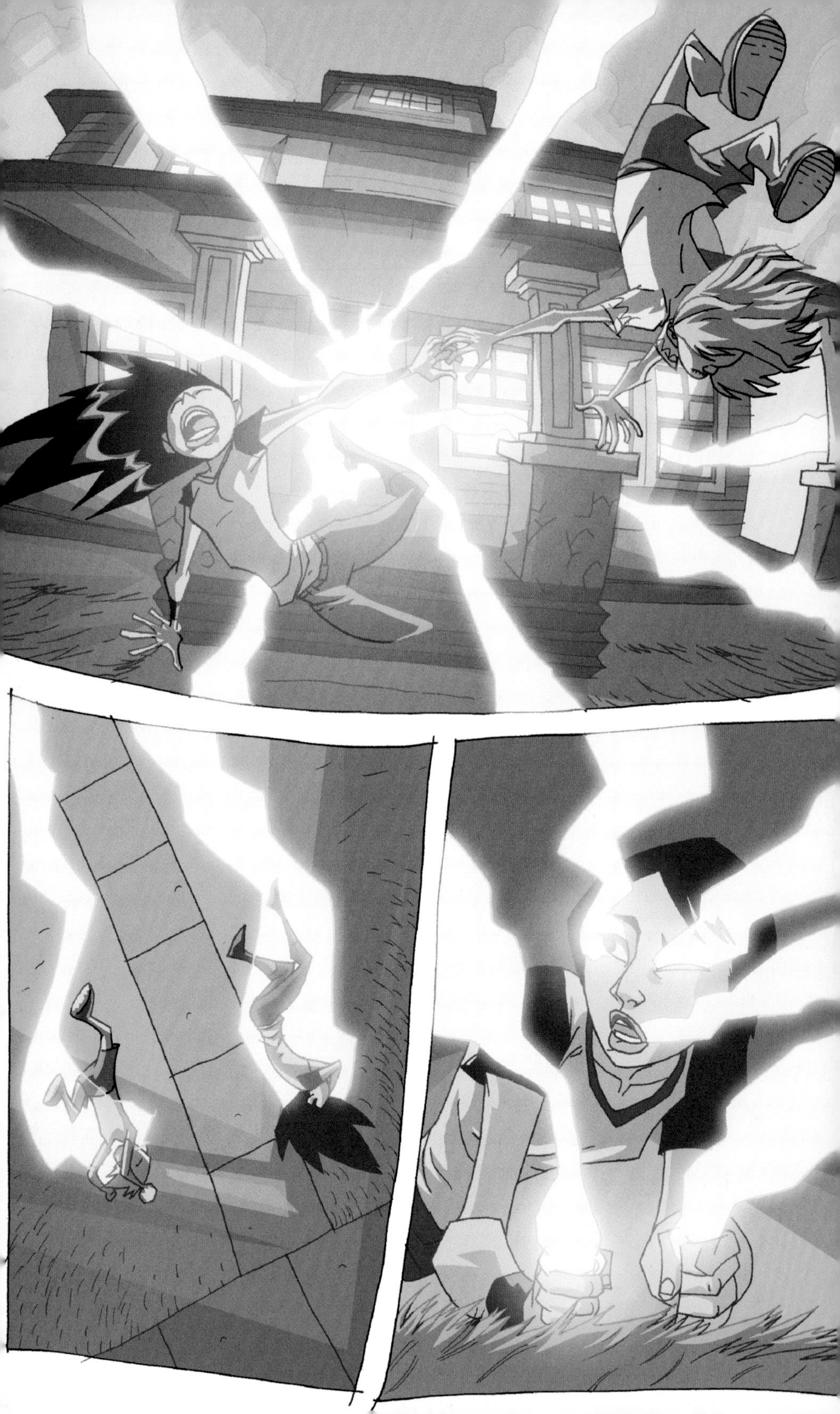

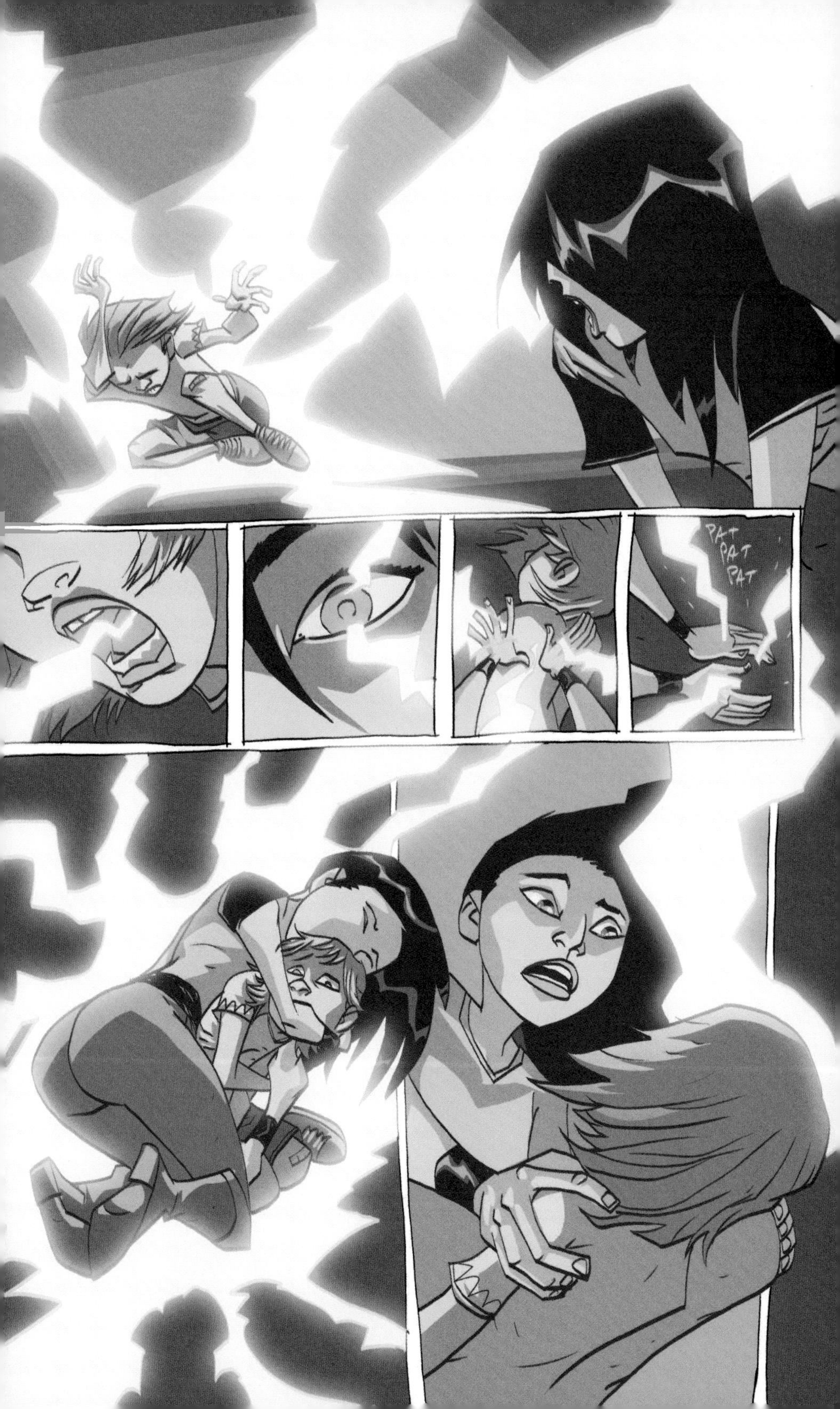
PAT
PAT
PAT

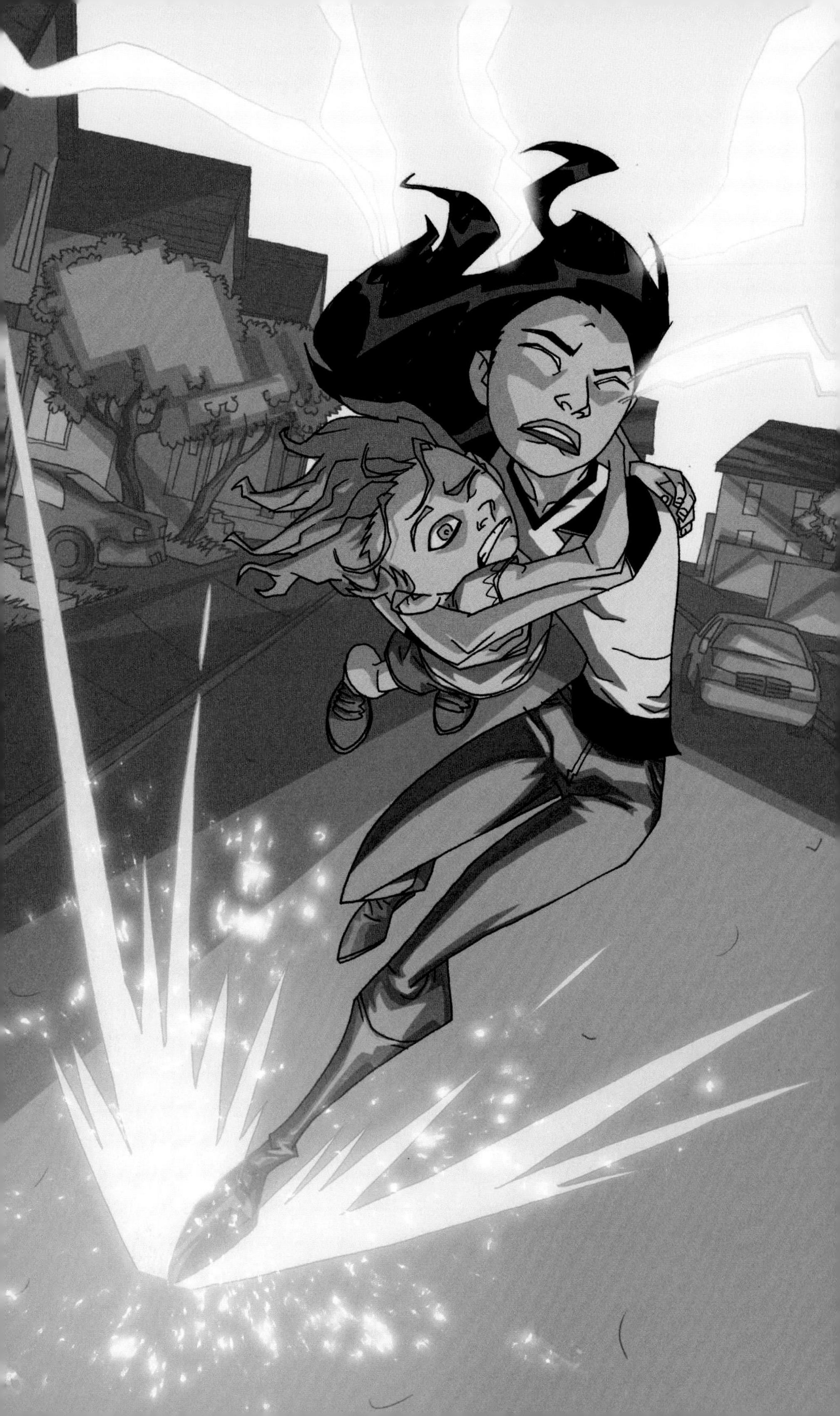

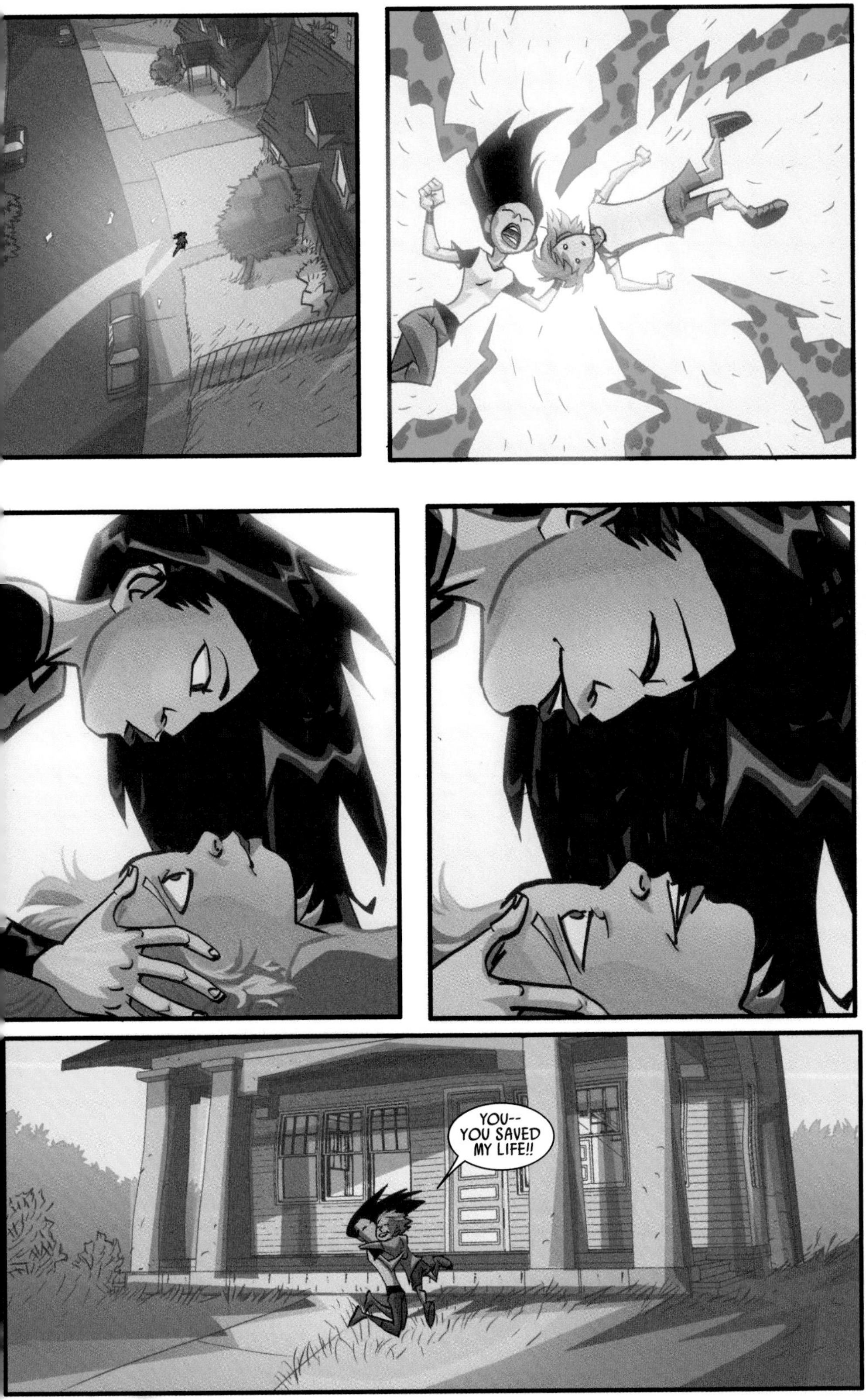
YOU--
YOU SAVED
MY LIFE!!

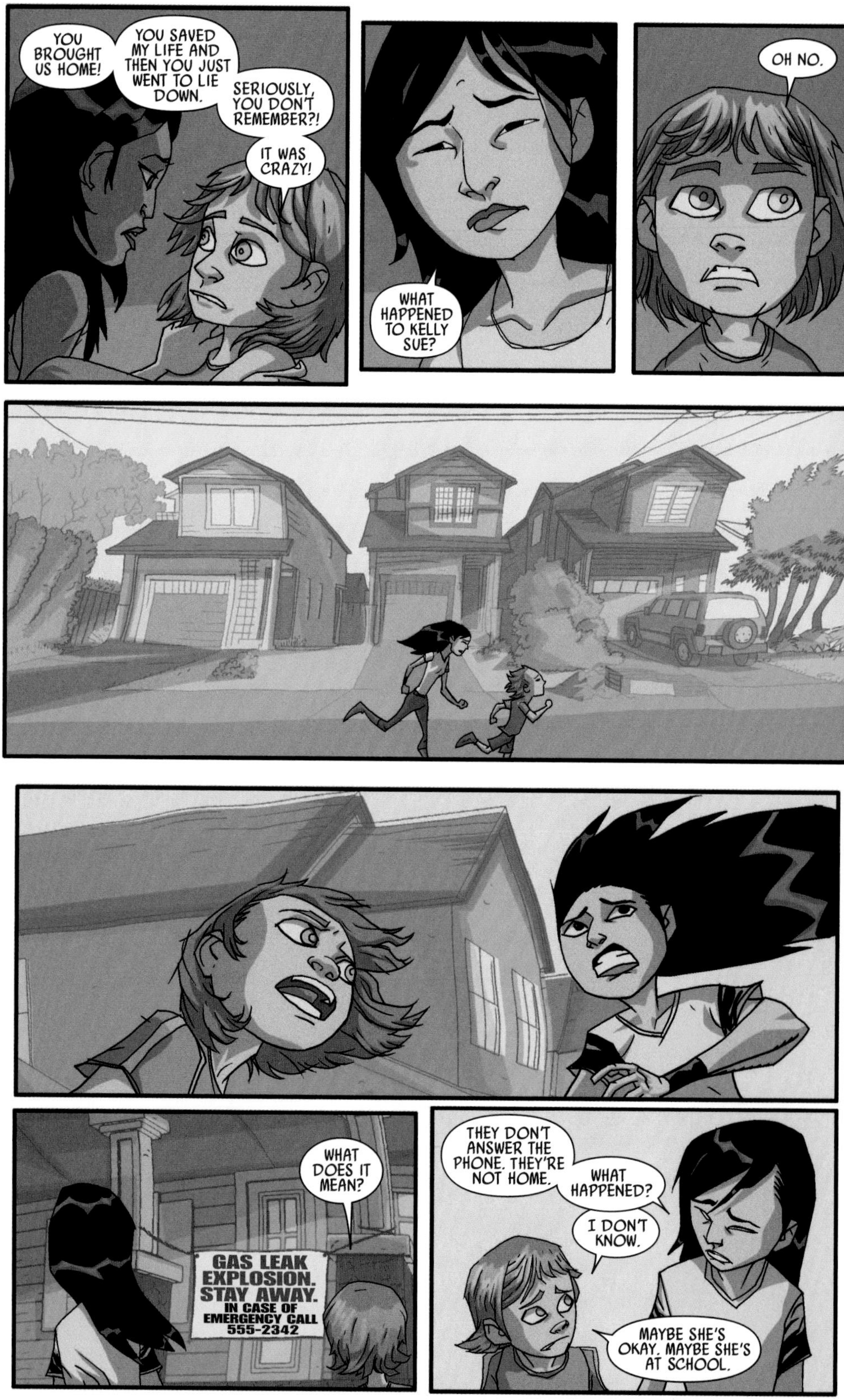
YOU BROUGHT US HOME!
YOU SAVED MY LIFE AND THEN YOU JUST WENT TO LIE DOWN.
SERIOUSLY, YOU DON'T REMEMBER?!
IT WAS CRAZY!
WHAT HAPPENED TO KELLY SUE?
OH NO.
WHAT DOES IT MEAN?
GAS LEAK EXPLOSION. STAY AWAY. IN CASE OF EMERGENCY CALL 555-2342
THEY DON'T ANSWER THE PHONE. THEY'RE NOT HOME.
WHAT HAPPENED?
I DON'T KNOW.
MAYBE SHE'S OKAY. MAYBE SHE'S AT SCHOOL.

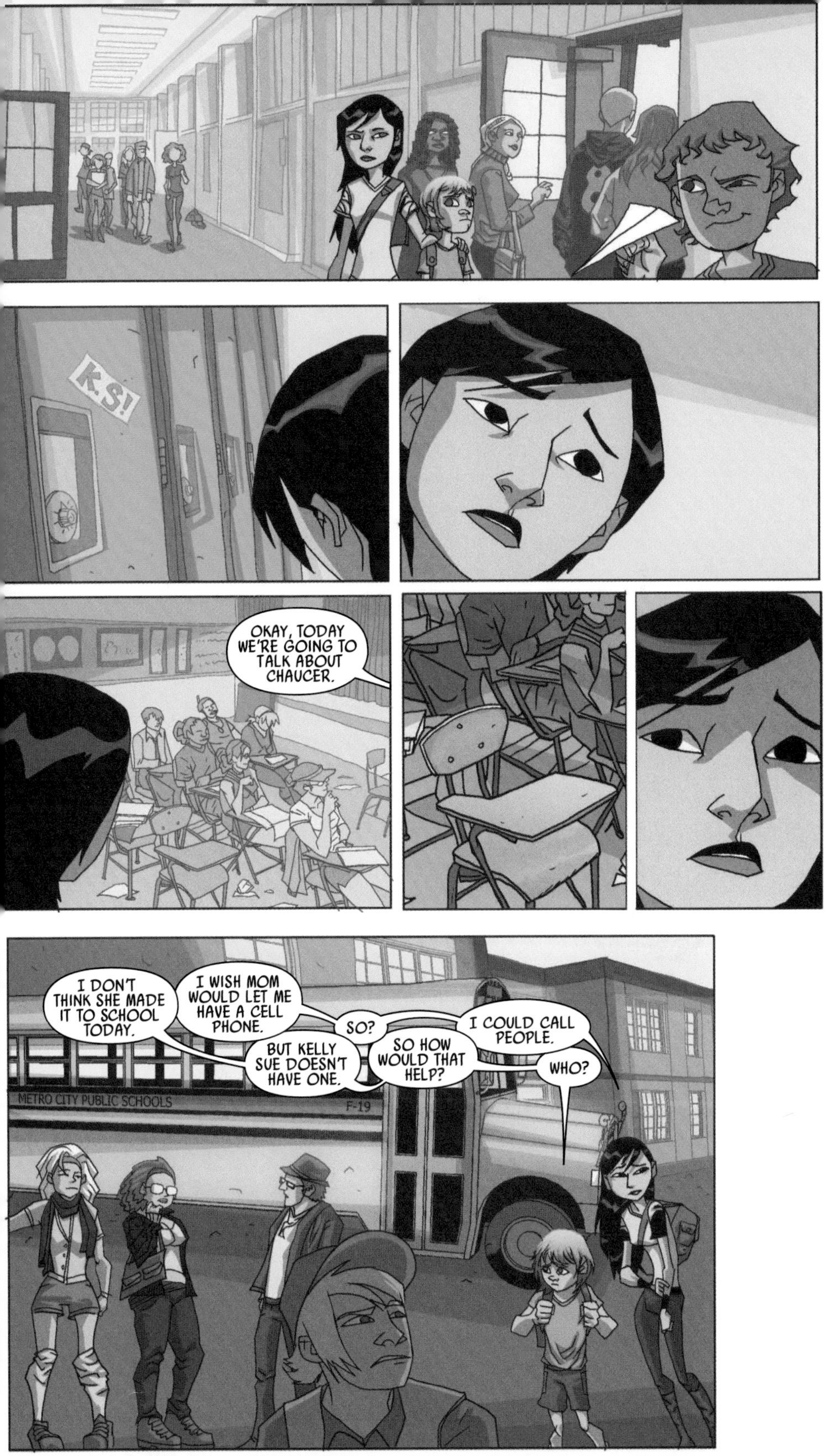
K.S!
OKAY, TODAY WE'RE GOING TO TALK ABOUT CHAUCER.
I DON'T THINK SHE MADE IT TO SCHOOL TODAY.
I WISH MOM WOULD LET ME HAVE A CELL PHONE.
BUT KELLY SUE DOESN'T HAVE ONE.
SO?
I COULD CALL PEOPLE.
SO HOW WOULD THAT HELP?
WHO?
METRO CITY PUBLIC SCHOOLS
F-19

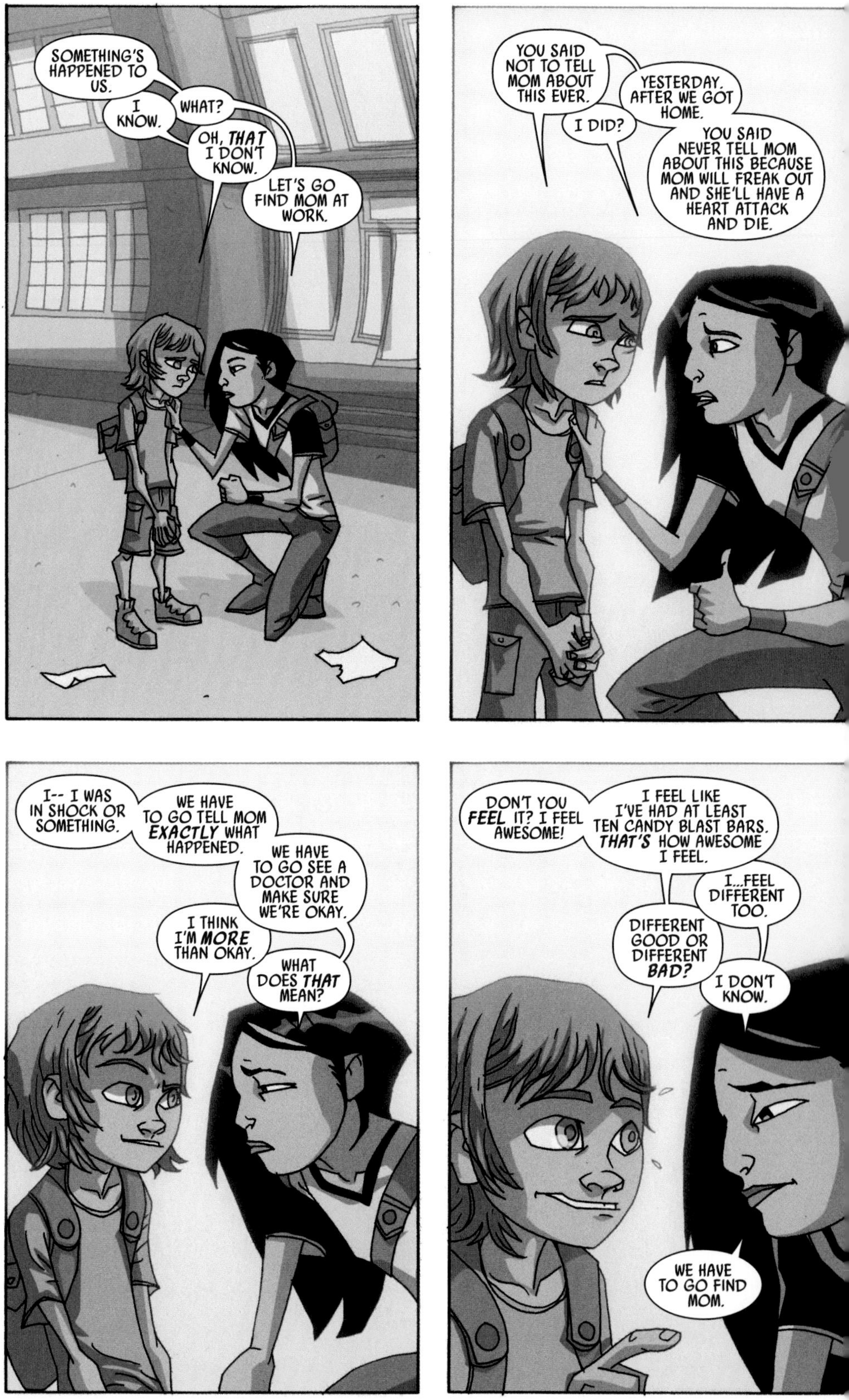
SOMETHING'S HAPPENED TO US.
WHAT?
I KNOW.
OH, *THAT* I DON'T KNOW.
LET'S GO FIND MOM AT WORK.
YOU SAID NOT TO TELL MOM ABOUT THIS EVER.
I DID?
YESTERDAY. AFTER WE GOT HOME.
YOU SAID NEVER TELL MOM ABOUT THIS BECAUSE MOM WILL FREAK OUT AND SHE'LL HAVE A HEART ATTACK AND DIE.
I-- I WAS IN SHOCK OR SOMETHING.
WE HAVE TO GO TELL MOM *EXACTLY* WHAT HAPPENED.
WE HAVE TO GO SEE A DOCTOR AND MAKE SURE WE'RE OKAY.
I THINK I'M *MORE* THAN OKAY.
WHAT DOES *THAT* MEAN?
DON'T YOU *FEEL* IT? I FEEL AWESOME!
I FEEL LIKE I'VE HAD AT LEAST TEN CANDY BLAST BARS. *THAT'S* HOW AWESOME I FEEL.
I...FEEL DIFFERENT TOO.
DIFFERENT GOOD OR DIFFERENT *BAD?*
I DON'T KNOW.
WE HAVE TO GO FIND MOM.

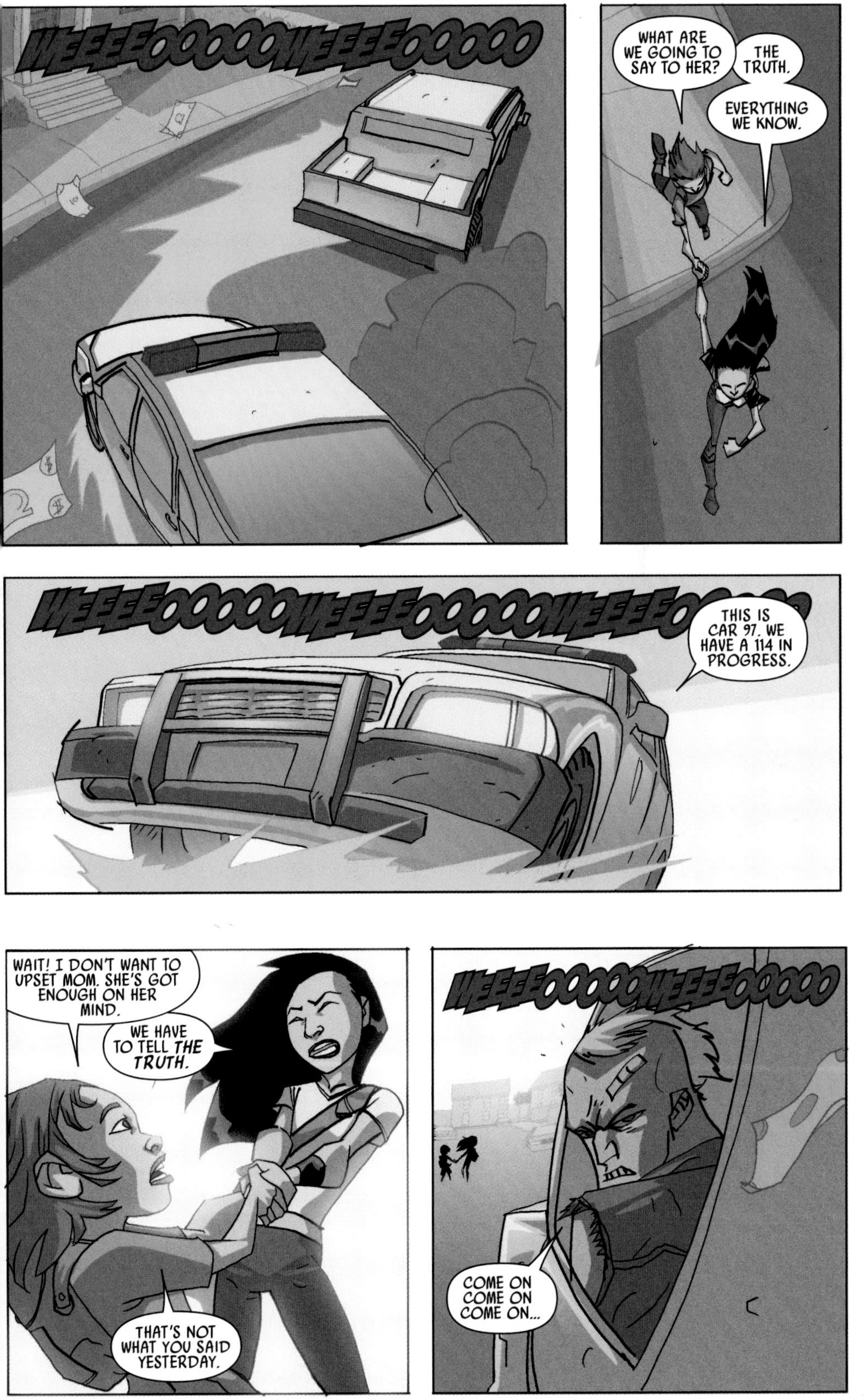
WEEEEOOOOOWEEEEOOOOO
WHAT ARE WE GOING TO SAY TO HER?
THE TRUTH.
EVERYTHING WE KNOW.
WEEEEOOOOOWEEEEOOOOOWEEEEOOOOO
THIS IS CAR 97. WE HAVE A 114 IN PROGRESS.
WAIT! I DON'T WANT TO UPSET MOM. SHE'S GOT ENOUGH ON HER MIND.
WE HAVE TO TELL *THE TRUTH*.
THAT'S NOT WHAT YOU SAID YESTERDAY.
WEEEEOOOOOWEEEEOOOOO
COME ON COME ON COME ON...

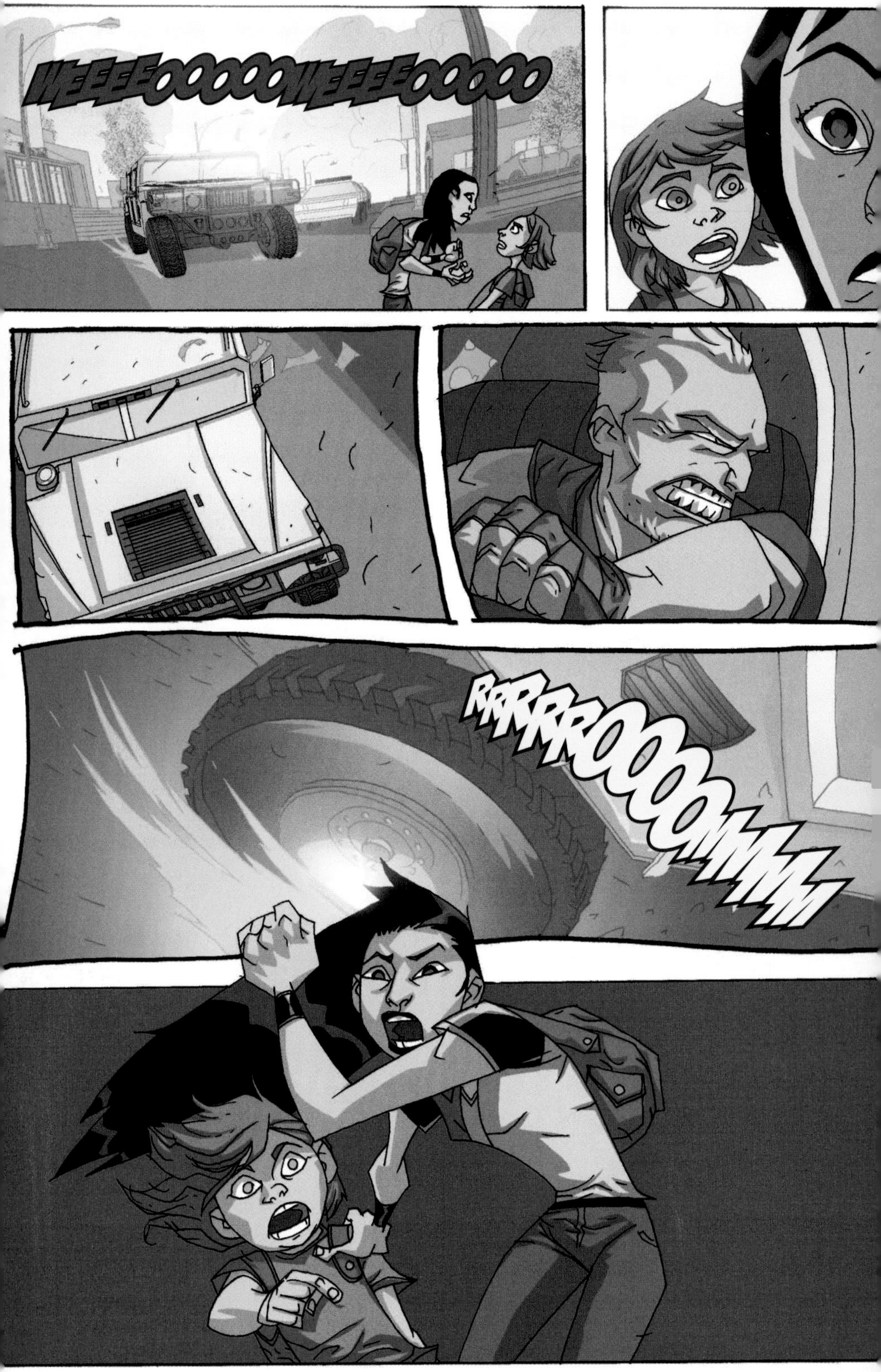
WEEEEOOOOOWEEEEOOOOO
RRRRROOOOOMMMM

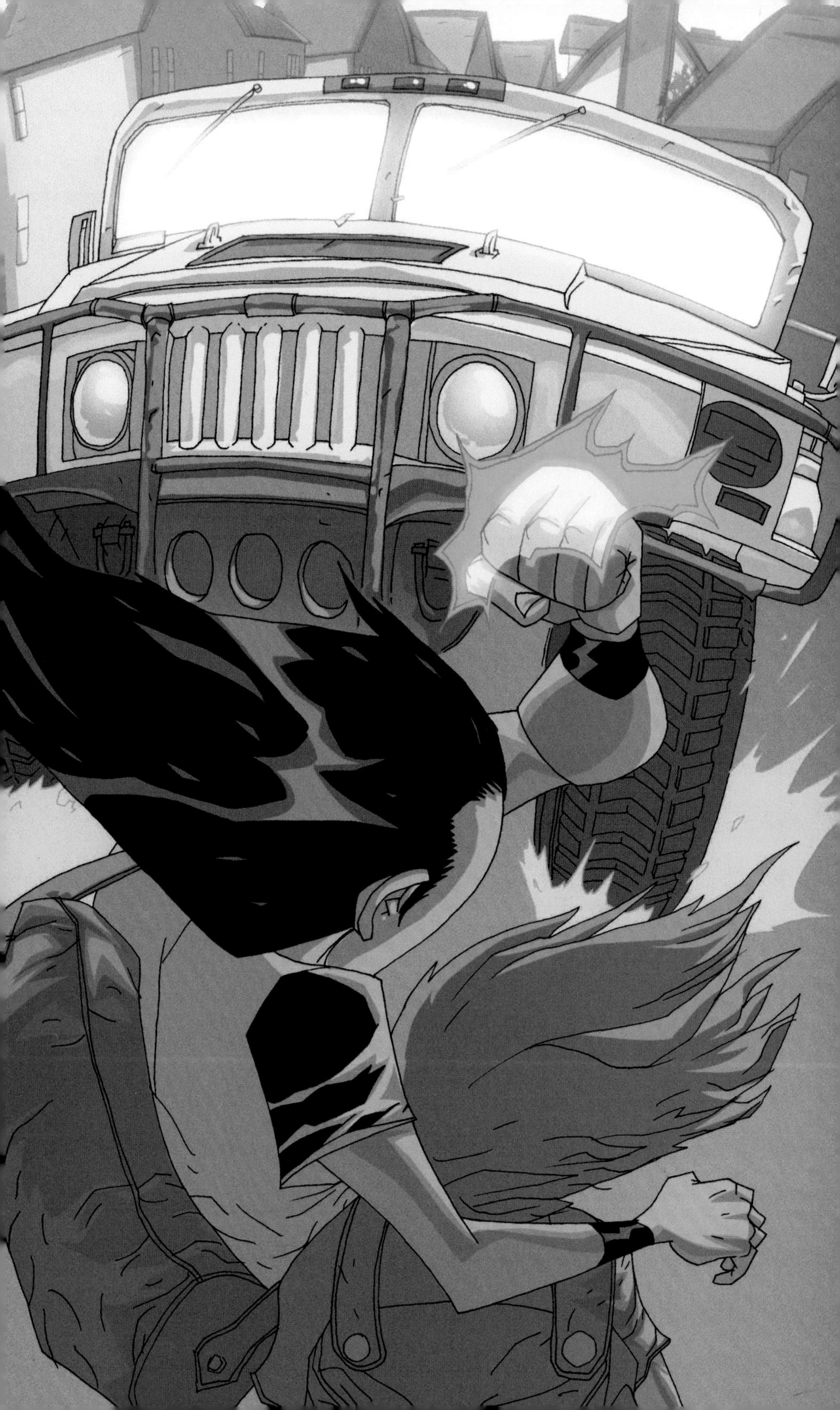

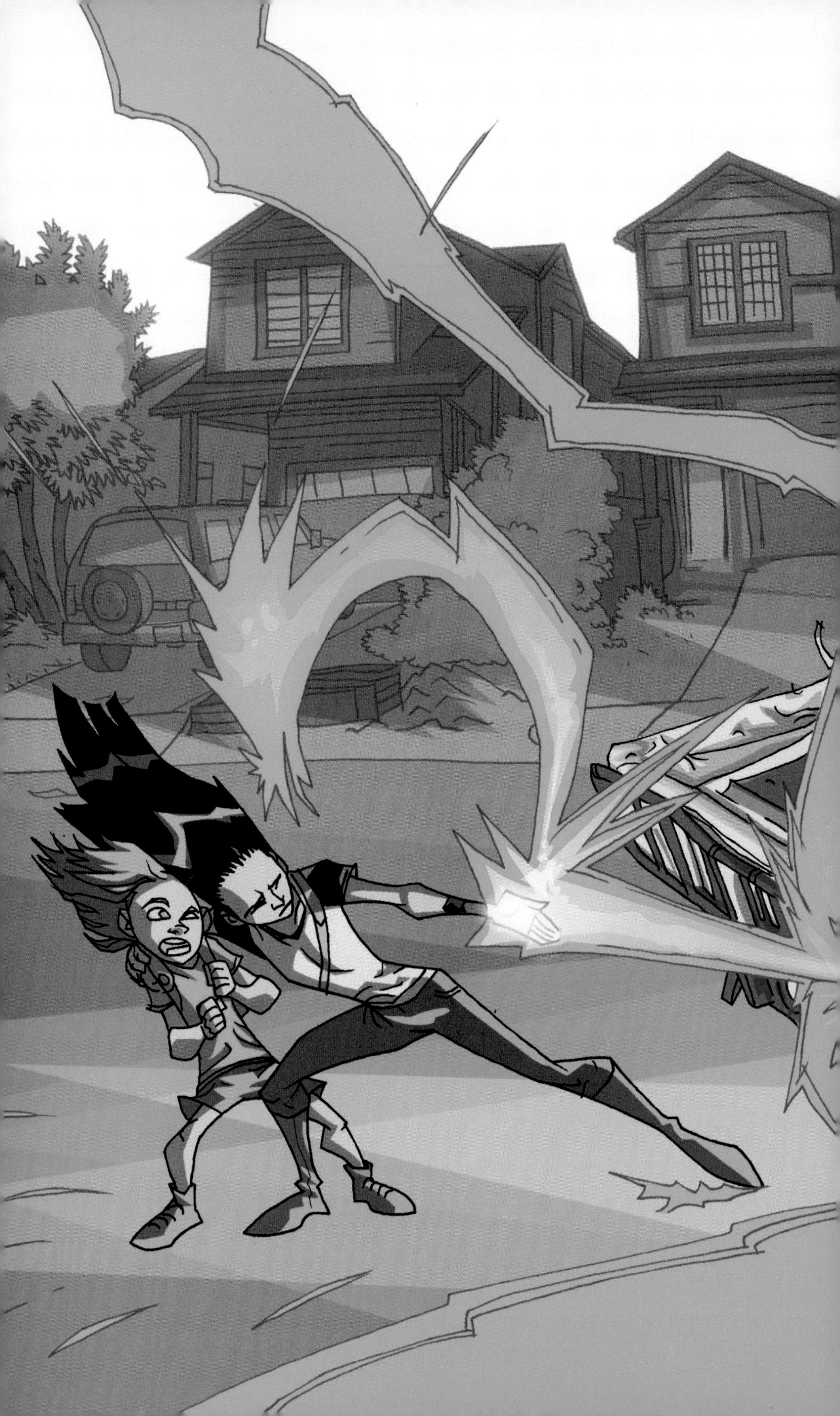

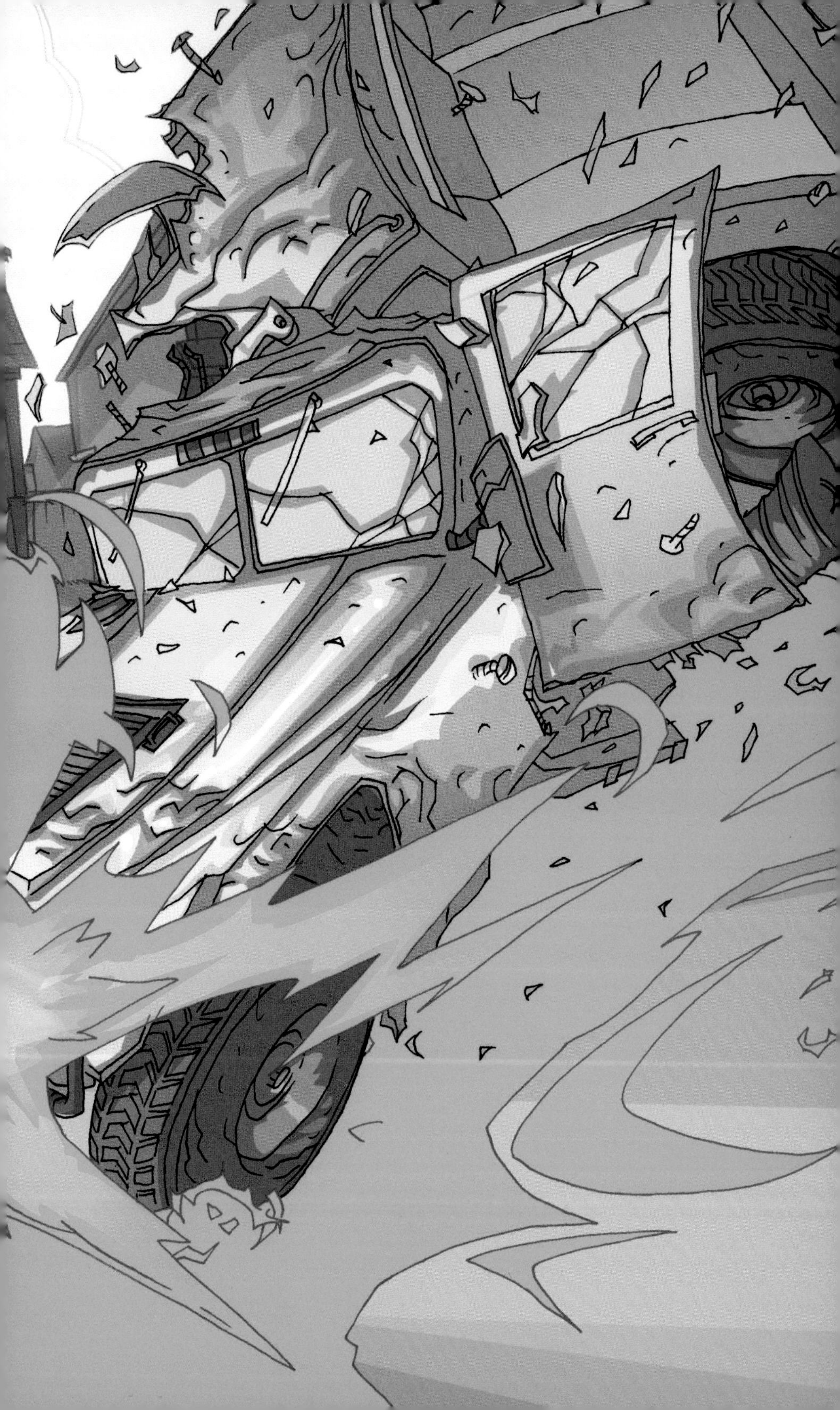

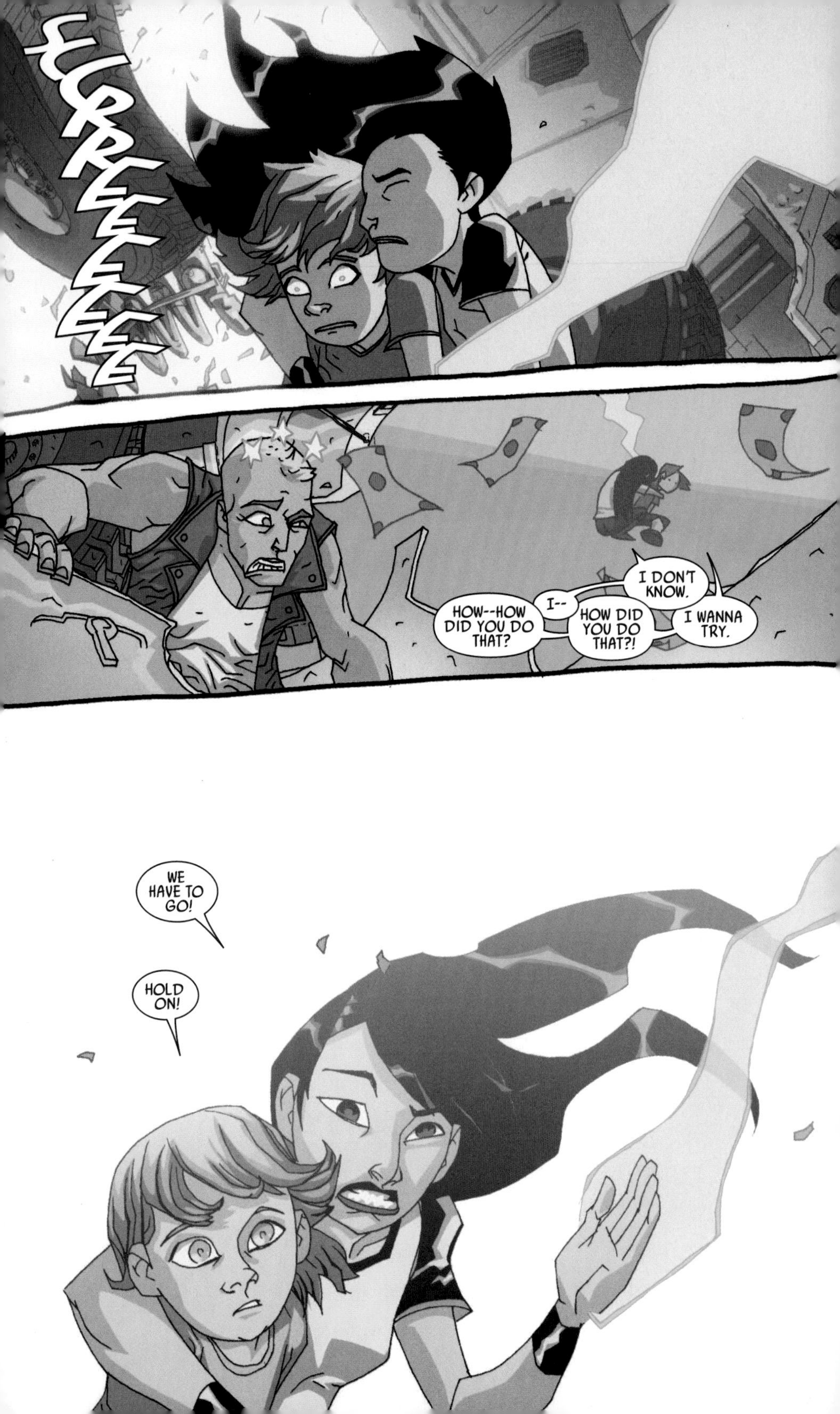
EEEREEEEEEE
HOW--HOW DID YOU DO THAT?
I--
HOW DID YOU DO THAT?!
I DON'T KNOW.
I WANNA TRY.
WE HAVE TO GO!
HOLD ON!

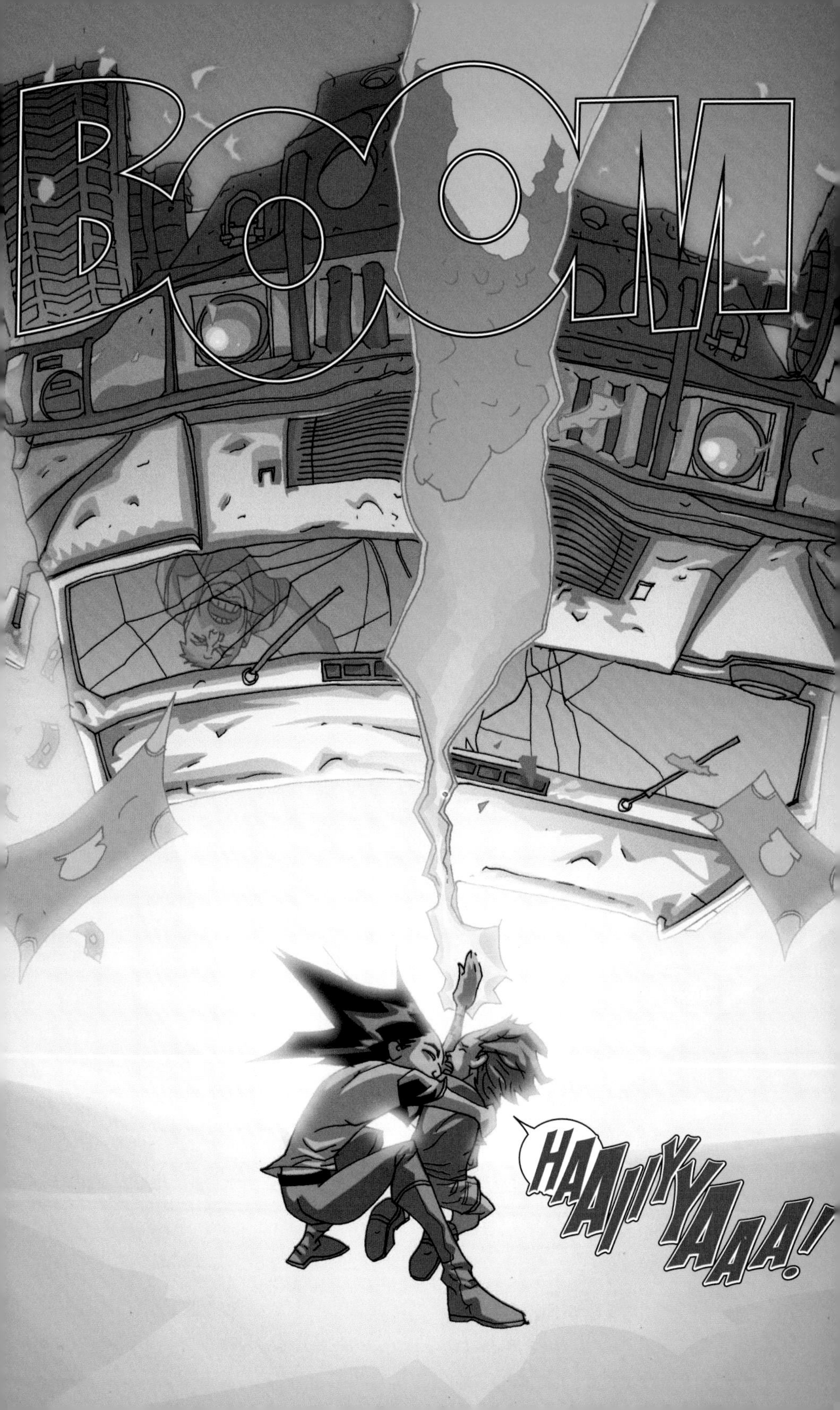
BOOM
HAAIIIYYAAA!

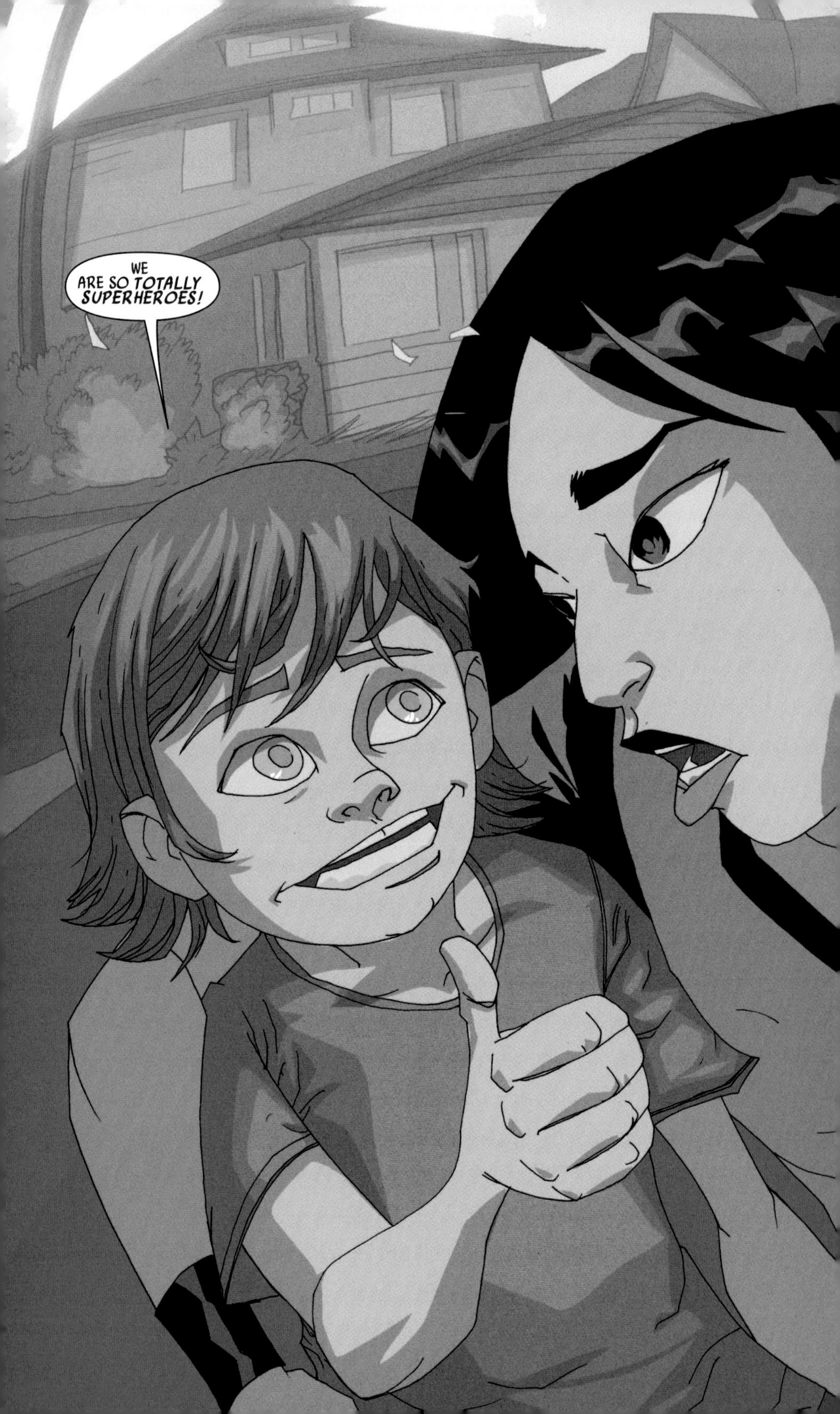
WE ARE SO TOTALLY SUPERHEROES!

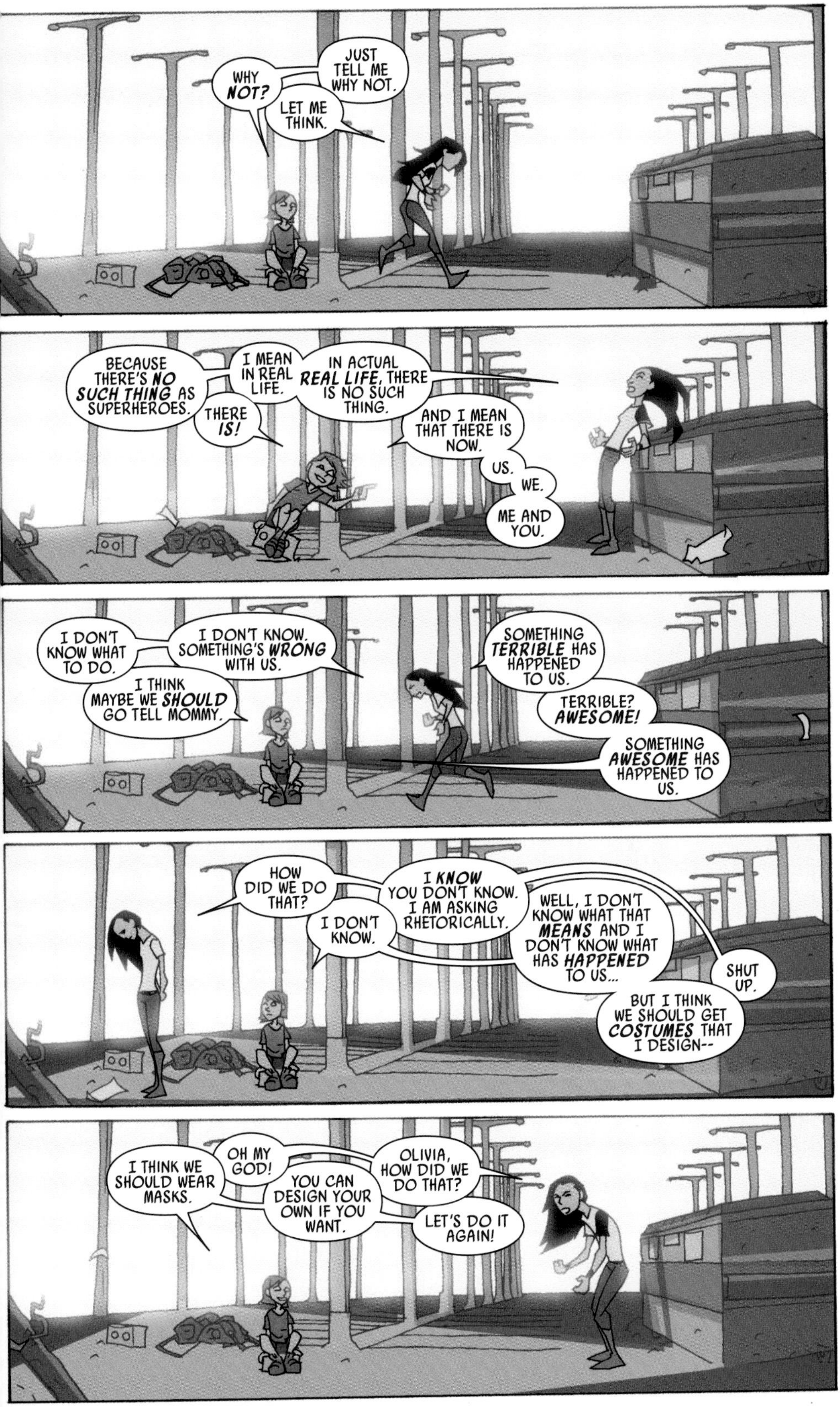
WHY NOT?
JUST TELL ME WHY NOT.
LET ME THINK.
BECAUSE THERE'S NO SUCH THING AS SUPERHEROES.
I MEAN IN REAL LIFE.
IN ACTUAL REAL LIFE, THERE IS NO SUCH THING.
THERE IS!
AND I MEAN THAT THERE IS NOW.
US.
WE.
ME AND YOU.
I DON'T KNOW WHAT TO DO.
I DON'T KNOW. SOMETHING'S WRONG WITH US.
I THINK MAYBE WE SHOULD GO TELL MOMMY.
SOMETHING TERRIBLE HAS HAPPENED TO US.
TERRIBLE? AWESOME!
SOMETHING AWESOME HAS HAPPENED TO US.
HOW DID WE DO THAT?
I DON'T KNOW.
I KNOW YOU DON'T KNOW. I AM ASKING RHETORICALLY.
WELL, I DON'T KNOW WHAT THAT MEANS AND I DON'T KNOW WHAT HAS HAPPENED TO US...
SHUT UP.
BUT I THINK WE SHOULD GET COSTUMES THAT I DESIGN--
I THINK WE SHOULD WEAR MASKS.
OH MY GOD!
OLIVIA, HOW DID WE DO THAT?
YOU CAN DESIGN YOUR OWN IF YOU WANT.
LET'S DO IT AGAIN!

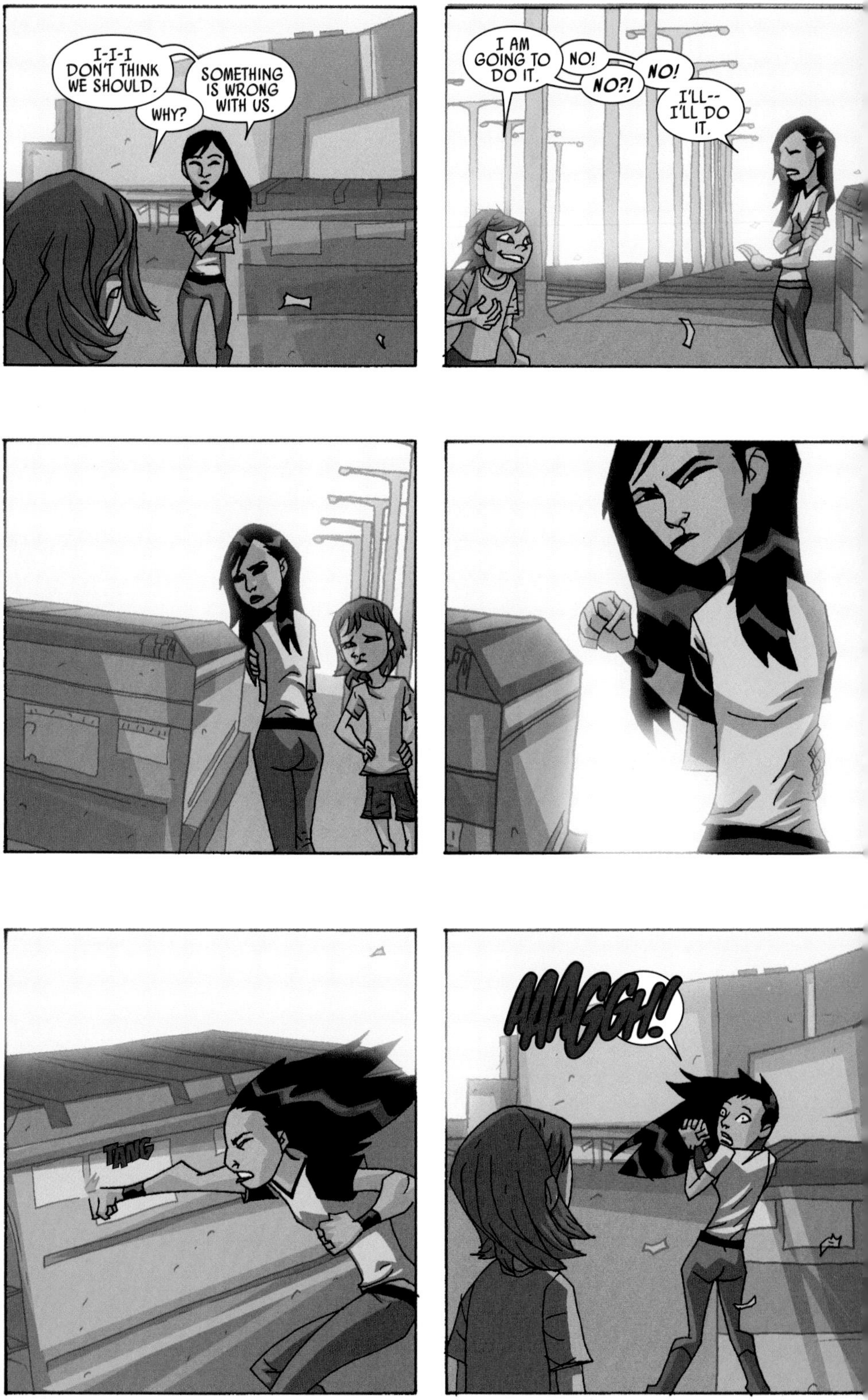
I-I-I DON'T THINK WE SHOULD.
WHY?
SOMETHING IS WRONG WITH US.
I AM GOING TO DO IT.
NO!
NO?!
NO!
I'LL-- I'LL DO IT.
TANG
AAAGGH!

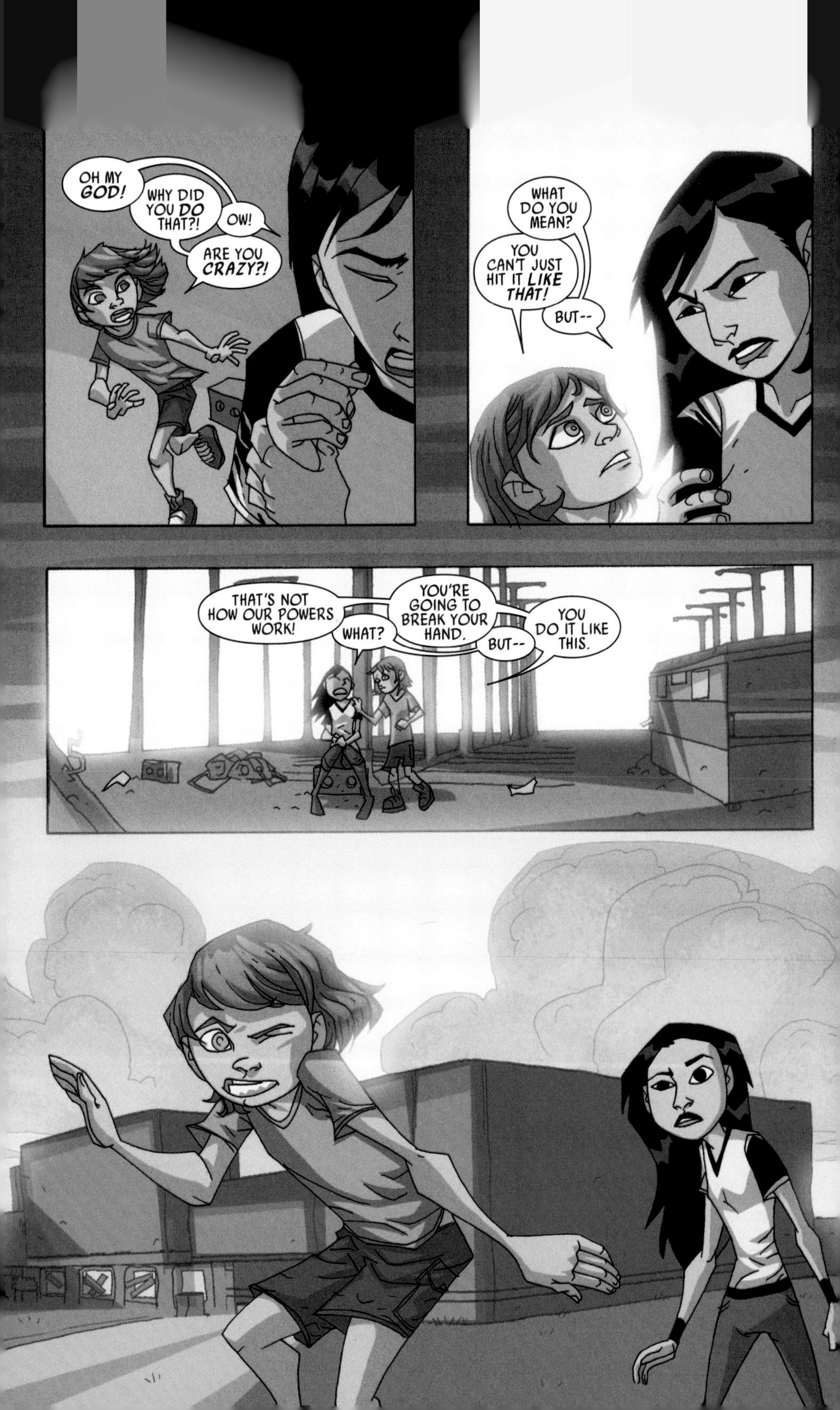
OH MY GOD!
WHY DID YOU DO THAT?!
OW!
ARE YOU CRAZY?!
WHAT DO YOU MEAN?
YOU CAN'T JUST HIT IT LIKE THAT!
BUT--
THAT'S NOT HOW OUR POWERS WORK!
WHAT?
YOU'RE GOING TO BREAK YOUR HAND.
BUT--
YOU DO IT LIKE THIS.

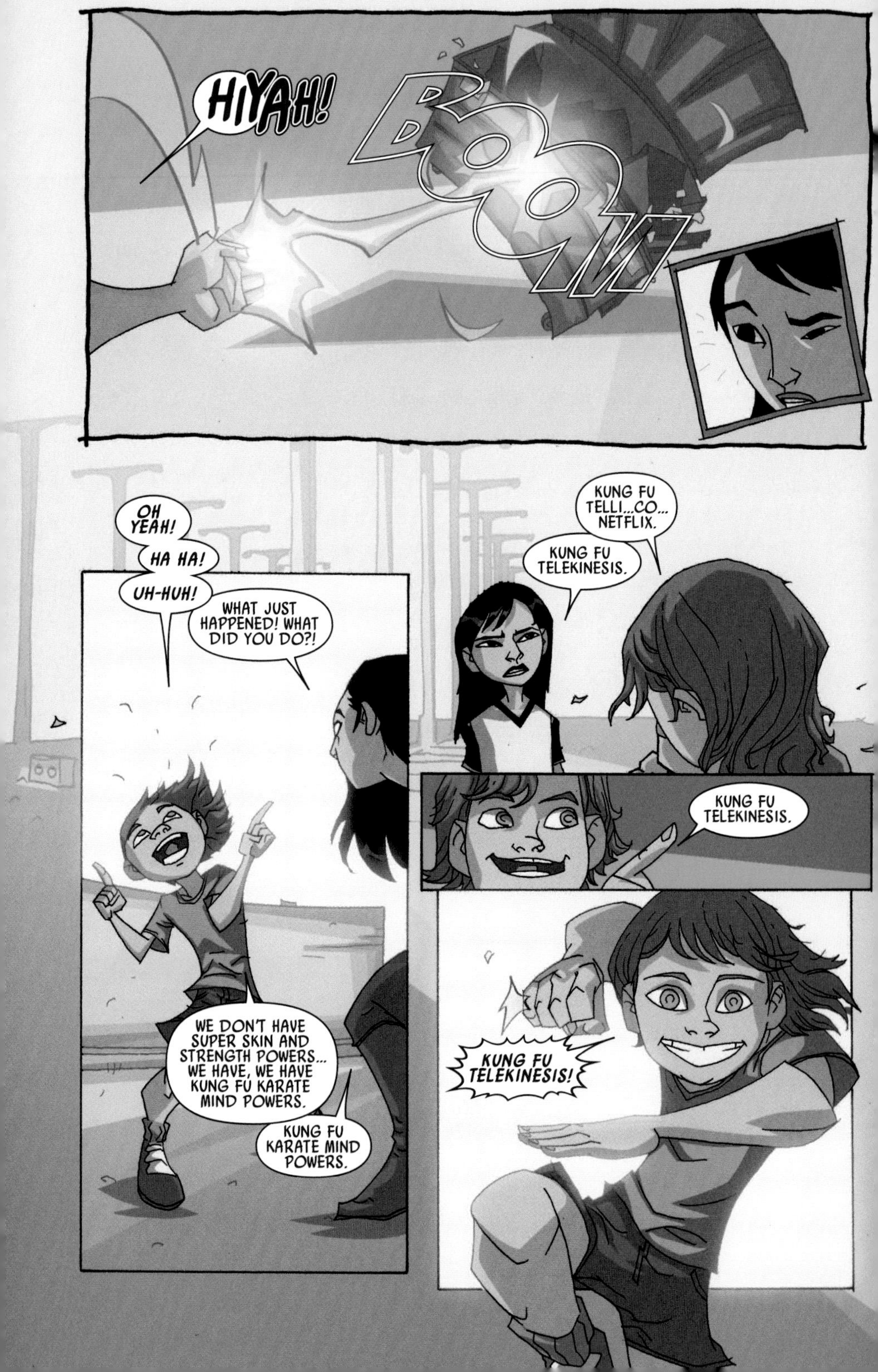
HIYAH!
BOOM
KUNG FU TELLI...CO... NETFLIX.
KUNG FU TELEKINESIS.
OH YEAH!
HA HA!
UH-HUH!
WHAT JUST HAPPENED! WHAT DID YOU DO?!
KUNG FU TELEKINESIS.
WE DON'T HAVE SUPER SKIN AND STRENGTH POWERS... WE HAVE, WE HAVE KUNG FU KARATE MIND POWERS.
KUNG FU KARATE MIND POWERS.
KUNG FU TELEKINESIS!

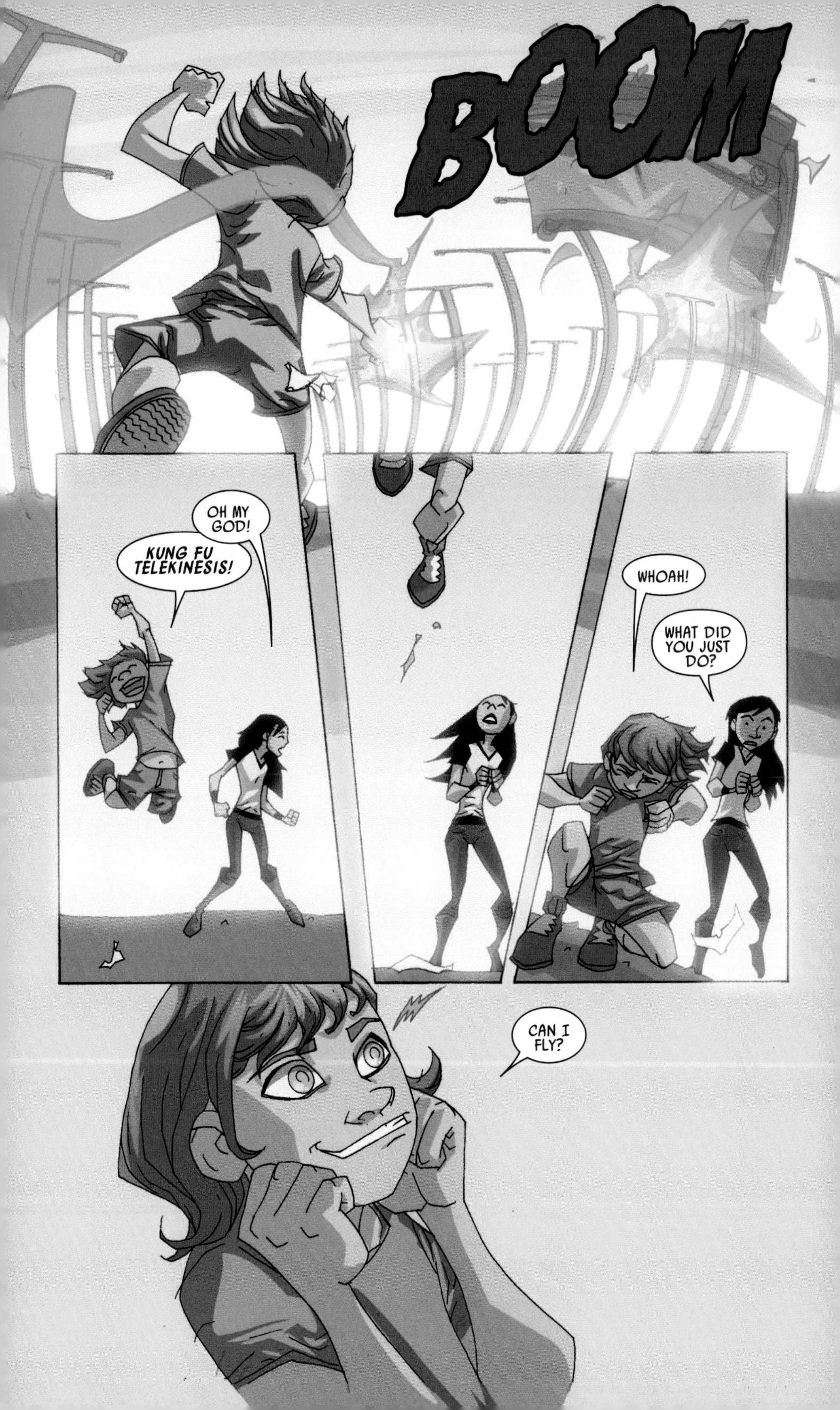

BOOM
OH MY GOD!
KUNG FU TELEKINESIS!
WHOAH!
WHAT DID YOU JUST DO?
CAN I FLY?

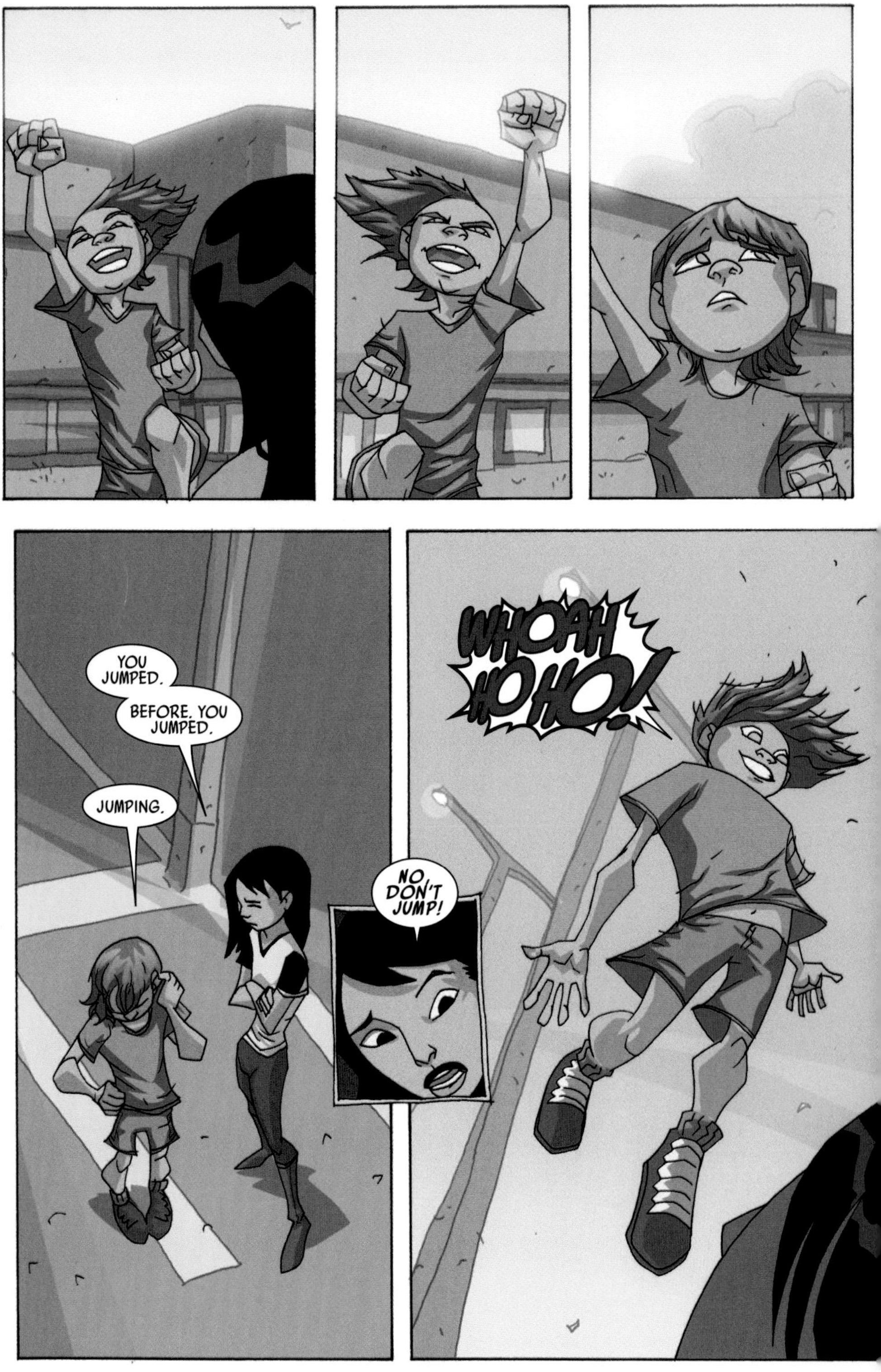
YOU JUMPED.
BEFORE. YOU JUMPED.
JUMPING.
NO DON'T JUMP!
WHOAH HO HO HO!

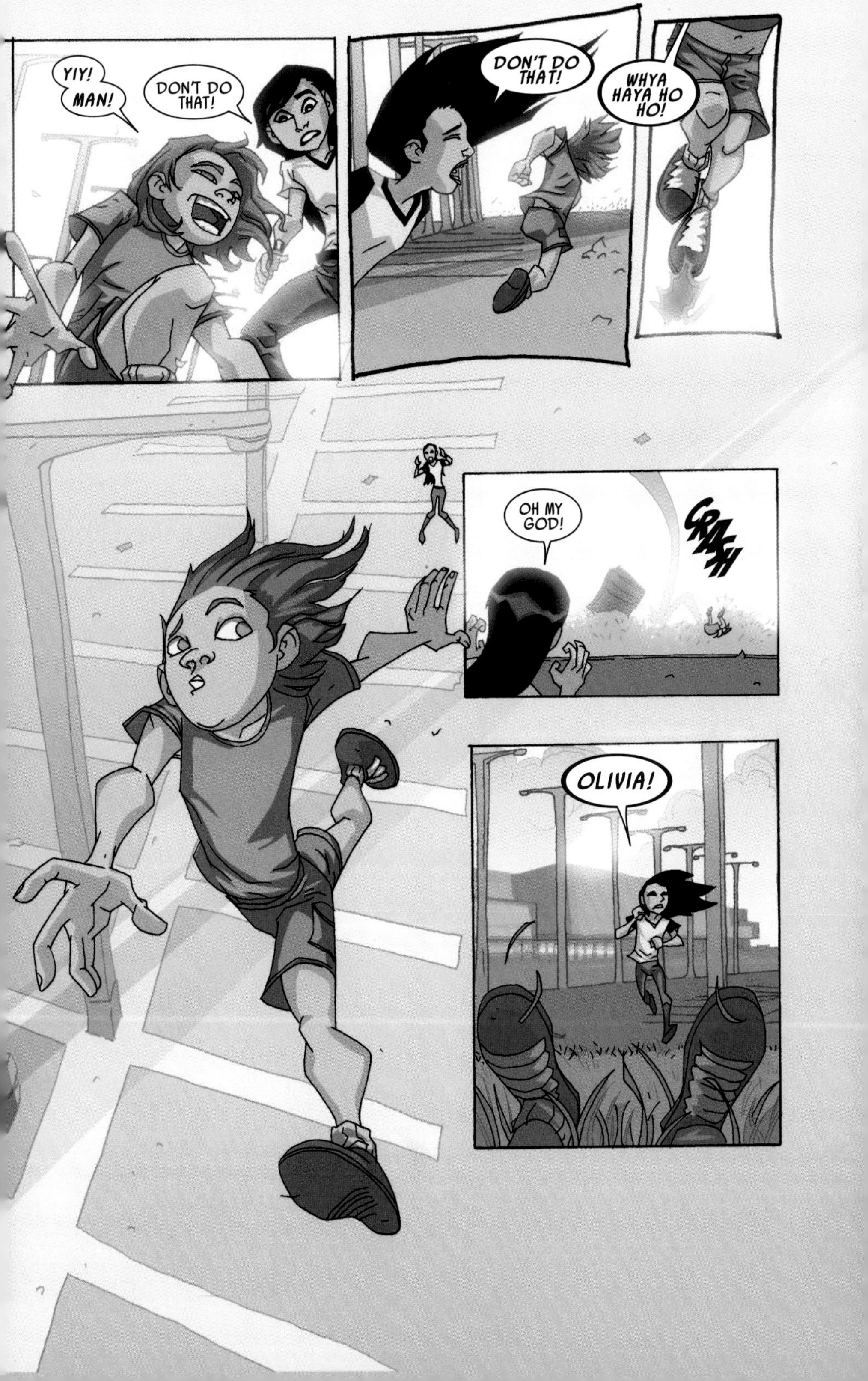
YIY! MAN!
DON'T DO THAT!
DON'T DO THAT!
WHYA HAYA HO HO!
OH MY GOD!
CRASH
OLIVIA!

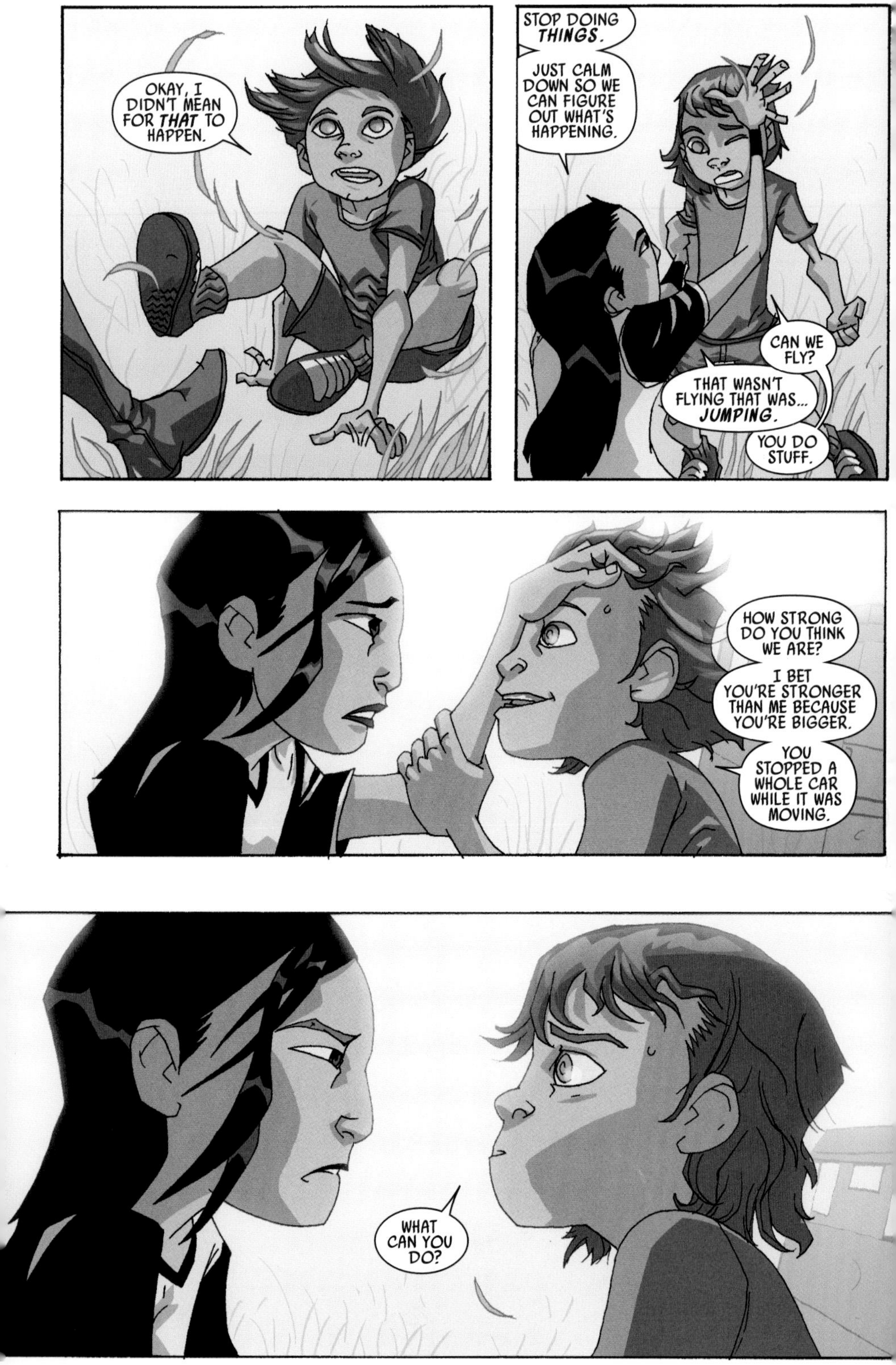
OKAY, I DIDN'T MEAN FOR *THAT* TO HAPPEN.
STOP DOING *THINGS*.
JUST CALM DOWN SO WE CAN FIGURE OUT WHAT'S HAPPENING.
CAN WE FLY?
THAT WASN'T FLYING THAT WAS... *JUMPING*.
YOU DO STUFF.
HOW STRONG DO YOU THINK WE ARE?
I BET YOU'RE STRONGER THAN ME BECAUSE YOU'RE BIGGER.
YOU STOPPED A WHOLE CAR WHILE IT WAS MOVING.
WHAT CAN YOU DO?

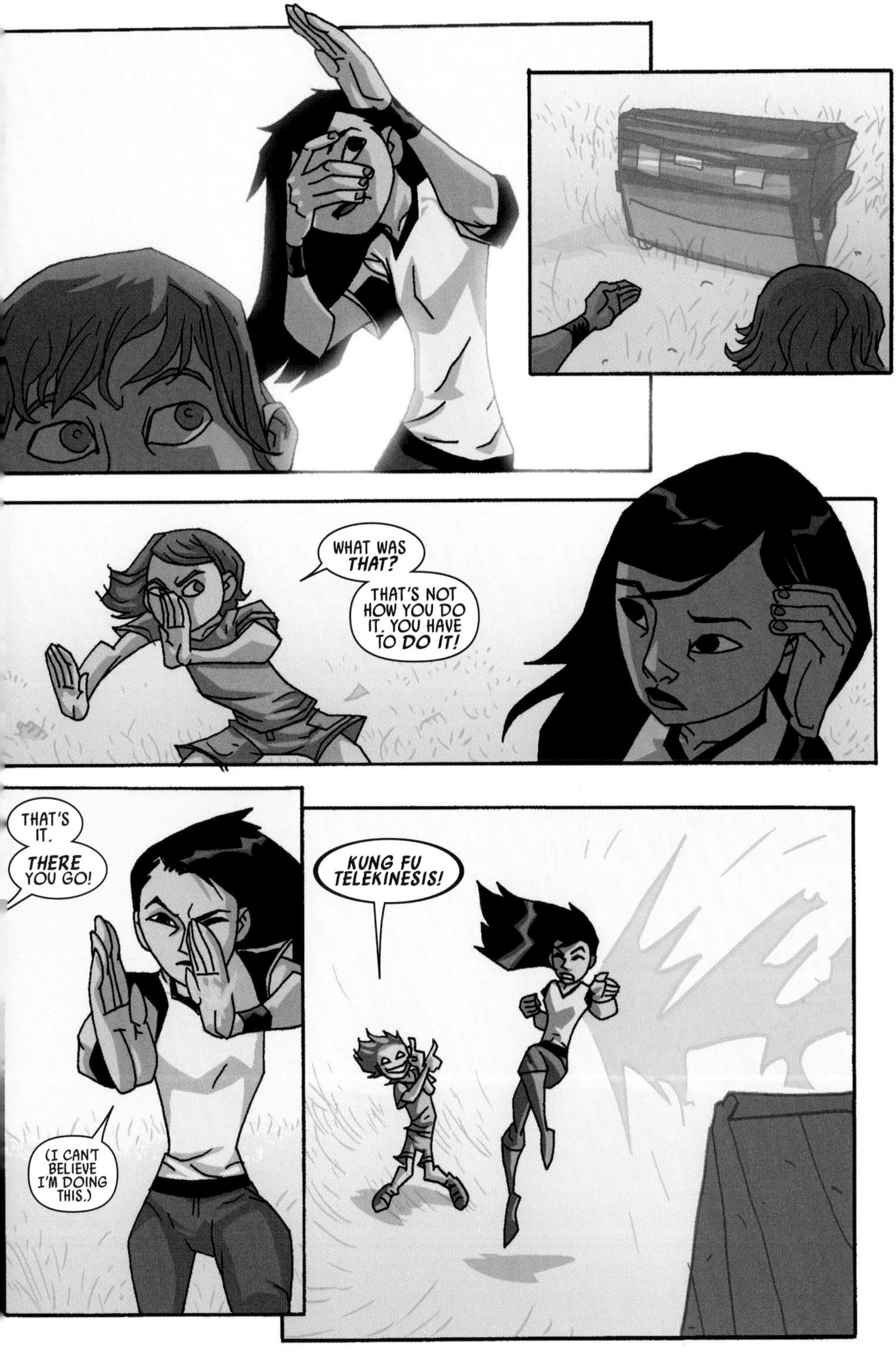
WHAT WAS THAT?
THAT'S NOT HOW YOU DO IT. YOU HAVE TO DO IT!
THAT'S IT.
THERE YOU GO!
(I CAN'T BELIEVE I'M DOING THIS.)
KUNG FU TELEKINESIS!

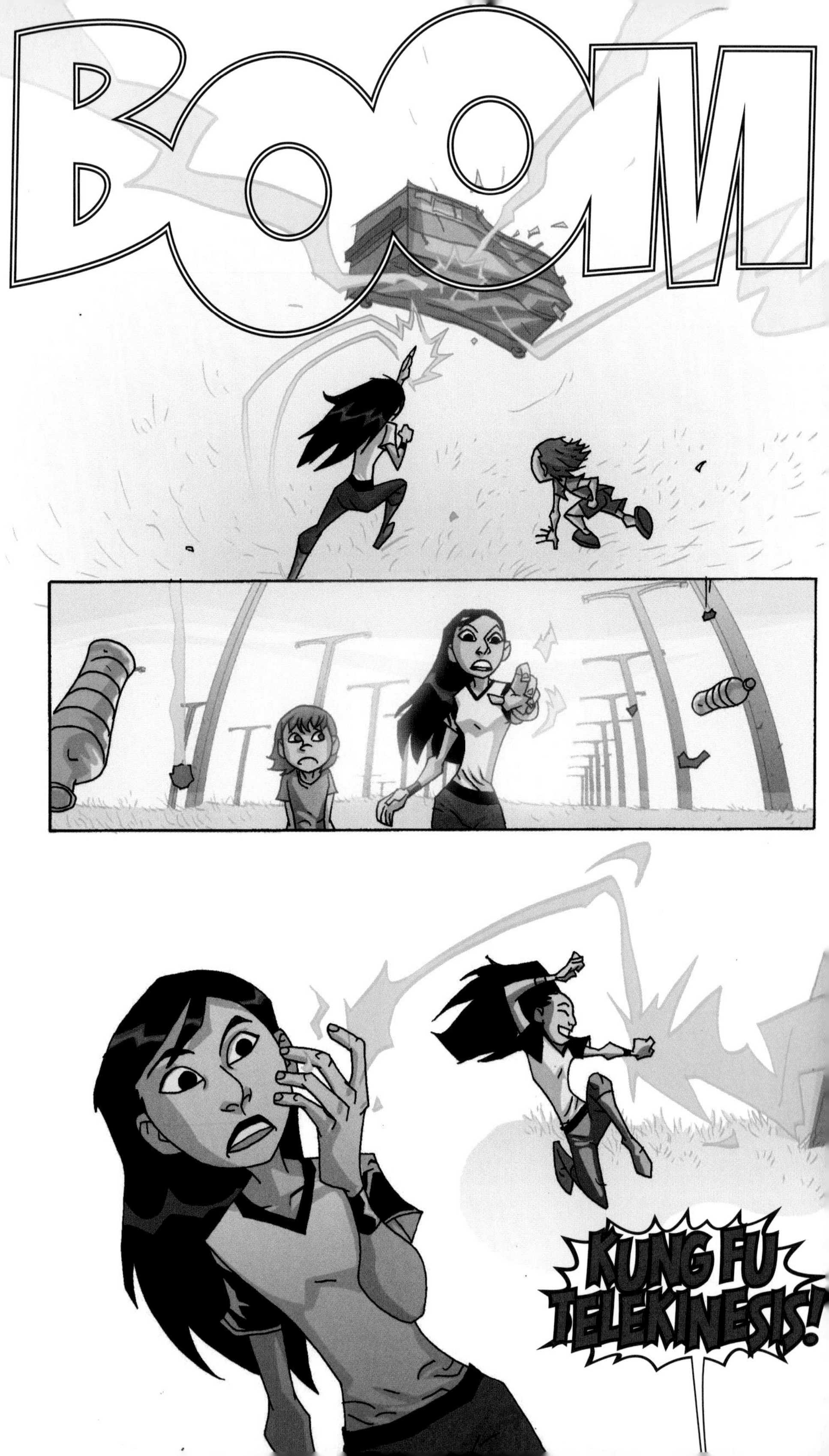
BOOM
KUNG FU TELEKINESIS!

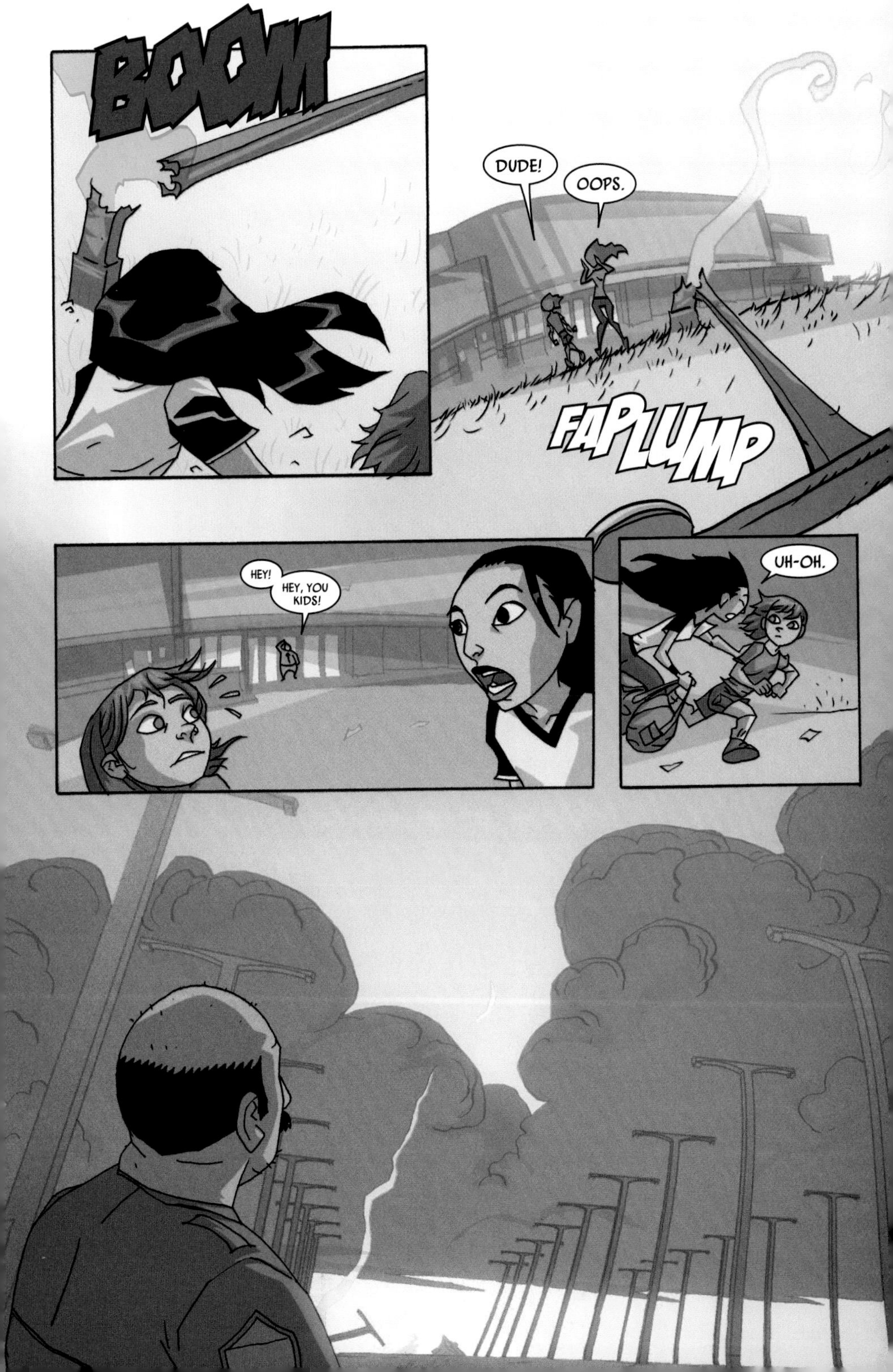
BOOM
DUDE!
OOPS.
FAPLUMP
HEY!
HEY, YOU KIDS!
UH-OH.

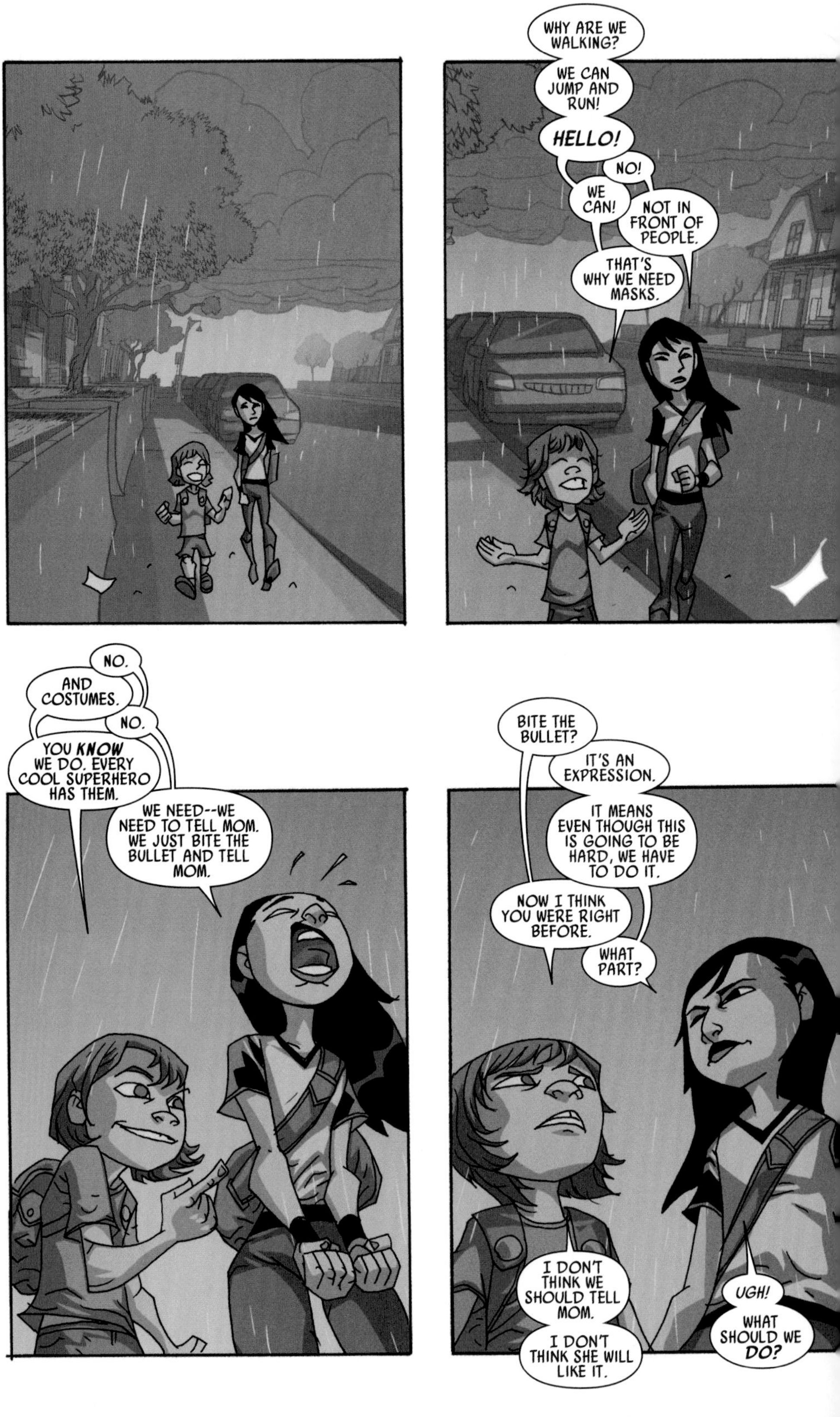

WHY ARE WE WALKING?
WE CAN JUMP AND RUN!
HELLO!
NO!
WE CAN!
NOT IN FRONT OF PEOPLE.
THAT'S WHY WE NEED MASKS.
AND COSTUMES.
NO.
NO.
YOU KNOW WE DO. EVERY COOL SUPERHERO HAS THEM.
WE NEED--WE NEED TO TELL MOM. WE JUST BITE THE BULLET AND TELL MOM.
BITE THE BULLET?
IT'S AN EXPRESSION.
IT MEANS EVEN THOUGH THIS IS GOING TO BE HARD, WE HAVE TO DO IT.
NOW I THINK YOU WERE RIGHT BEFORE.
WHAT PART?
I DON'T THINK WE SHOULD TELL MOM.
I DON'T THINK SHE WILL LIKE IT.
UGH!
WHAT SHOULD WE DO?

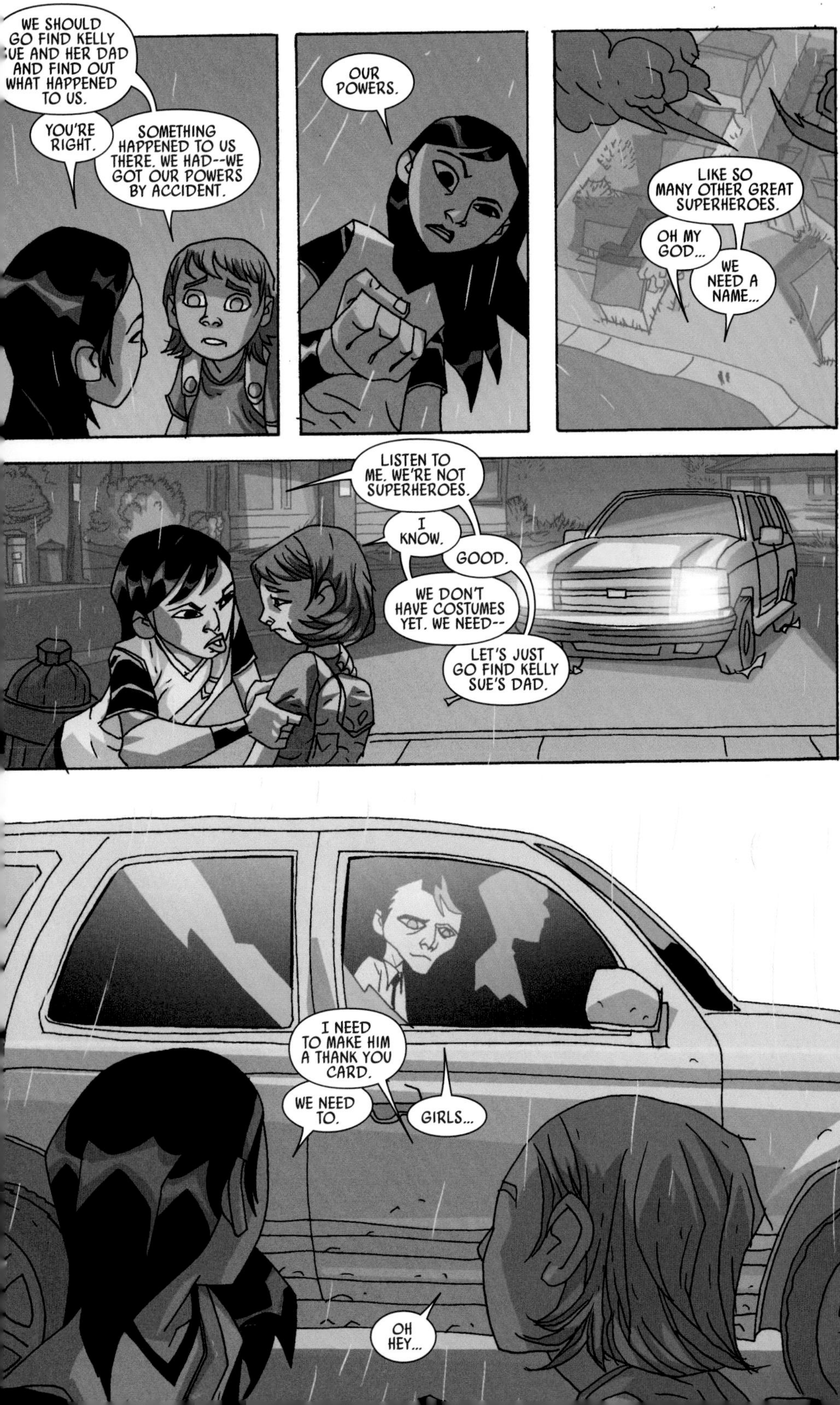
WE SHOULD GO FIND KELLY SUE AND HER DAD AND FIND OUT WHAT HAPPENED TO US.
YOU'RE RIGHT.
SOMETHING HAPPENED TO US THERE. WE HAD--WE GOT OUR POWERS BY ACCIDENT.
OUR POWERS.
LIKE SO MANY OTHER GREAT SUPERHEROES.
OH MY GOD...
WE NEED A NAME...
LISTEN TO ME. WE'RE NOT SUPERHEROES.
I KNOW.
GOOD.
WE DON'T HAVE COSTUMES YET. WE NEED--
LET'S JUST GO FIND KELLY SUE'S DAD.
I NEED TO MAKE HIM A THANK YOU CARD.
WE NEED TO.
GIRLS...
OH HEY...

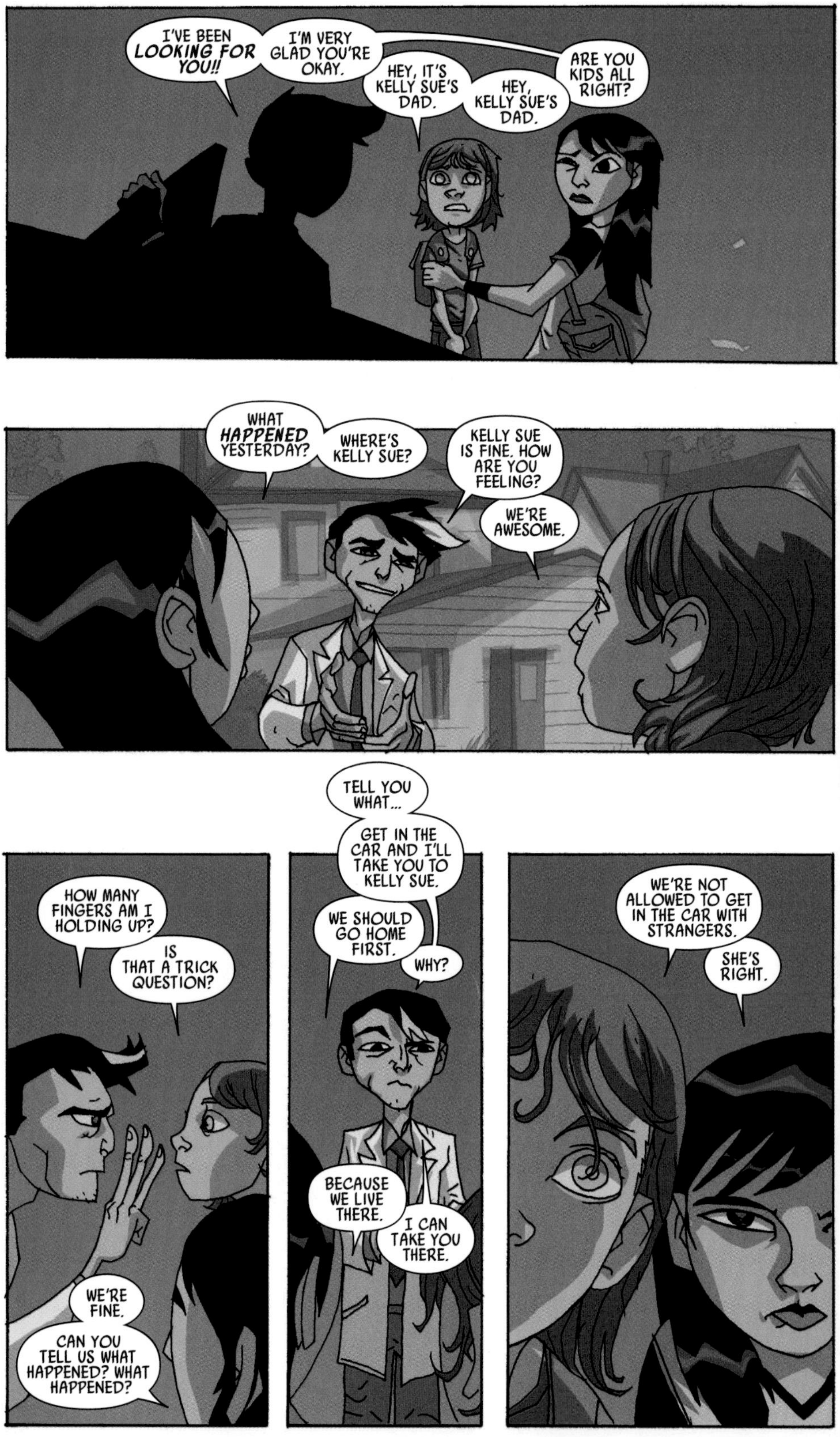

I'VE BEEN LOOKING FOR YOU!!
I'M VERY GLAD YOU'RE OKAY.
ARE YOU KIDS ALL RIGHT?
HEY, IT'S KELLY SUE'S DAD.
HEY, KELLY SUE'S DAD.
WHAT HAPPENED YESTERDAY?
WHERE'S KELLY SUE?
KELLY SUE IS FINE. HOW ARE YOU FEELING?
WE'RE AWESOME.
HOW MANY FINGERS AM I HOLDING UP?
IS THAT A TRICK QUESTION?
WE'RE FINE.
CAN YOU TELL US WHAT HAPPENED? WHAT HAPPENED?
TELL YOU WHAT...
GET IN THE CAR AND I'LL TAKE YOU TO KELLY SUE.
WE SHOULD GO HOME FIRST.
WHY?
BECAUSE WE LIVE THERE.
I CAN TAKE YOU THERE.
WE'RE NOT ALLOWED TO GET IN THE CAR WITH STRANGERS.
SHE'S RIGHT.

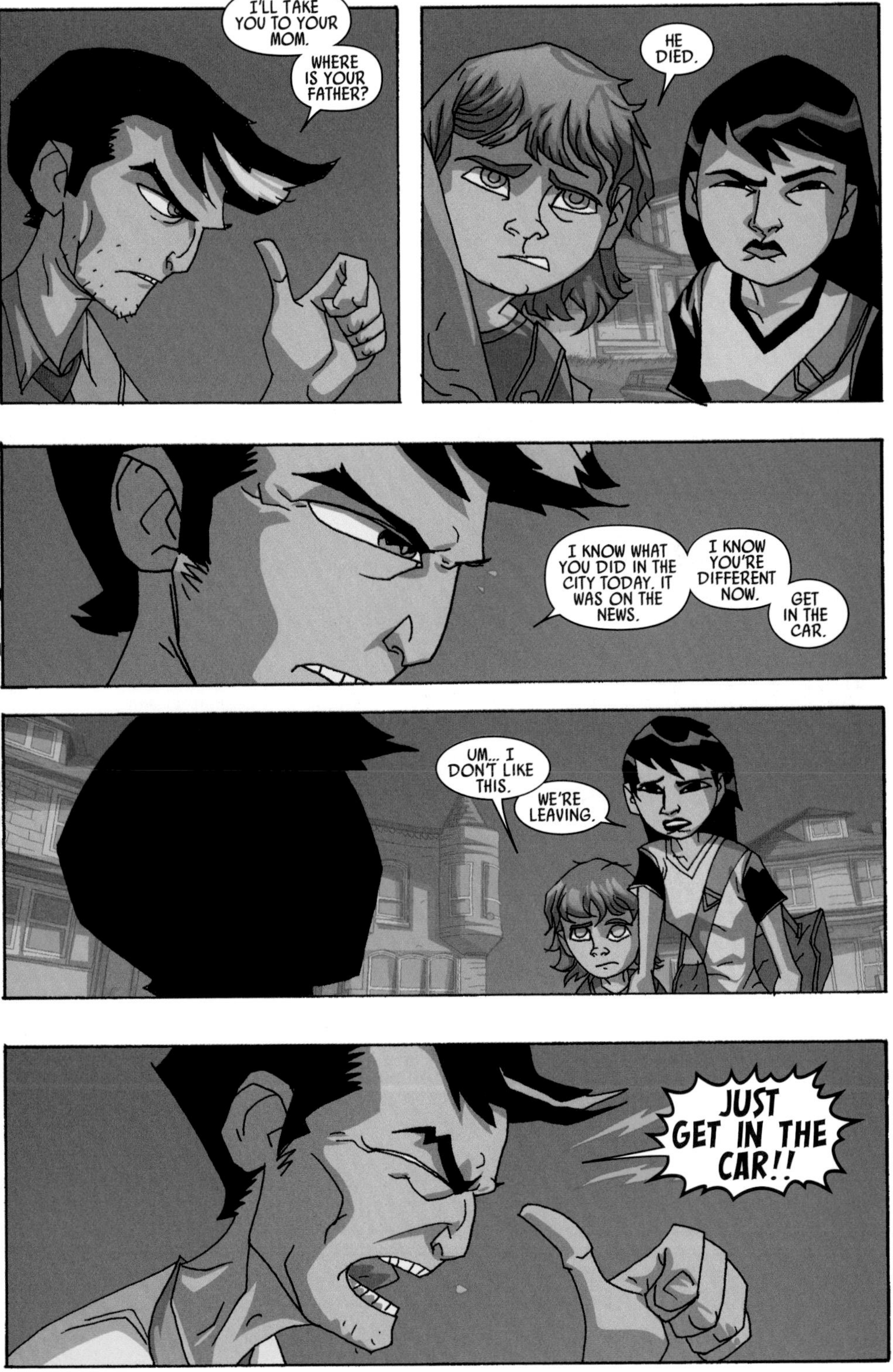
I'LL TAKE YOU TO YOUR MOM.
WHERE IS YOUR FATHER?
HE DIED.
I KNOW WHAT YOU DID IN THE CITY TODAY. IT WAS ON THE NEWS.
I KNOW YOU'RE DIFFERENT NOW.
GET IN THE CAR.
UM... I DON'T LIKE THIS.
WE'RE LEAVING.
JUST GET IN THE CAR!!

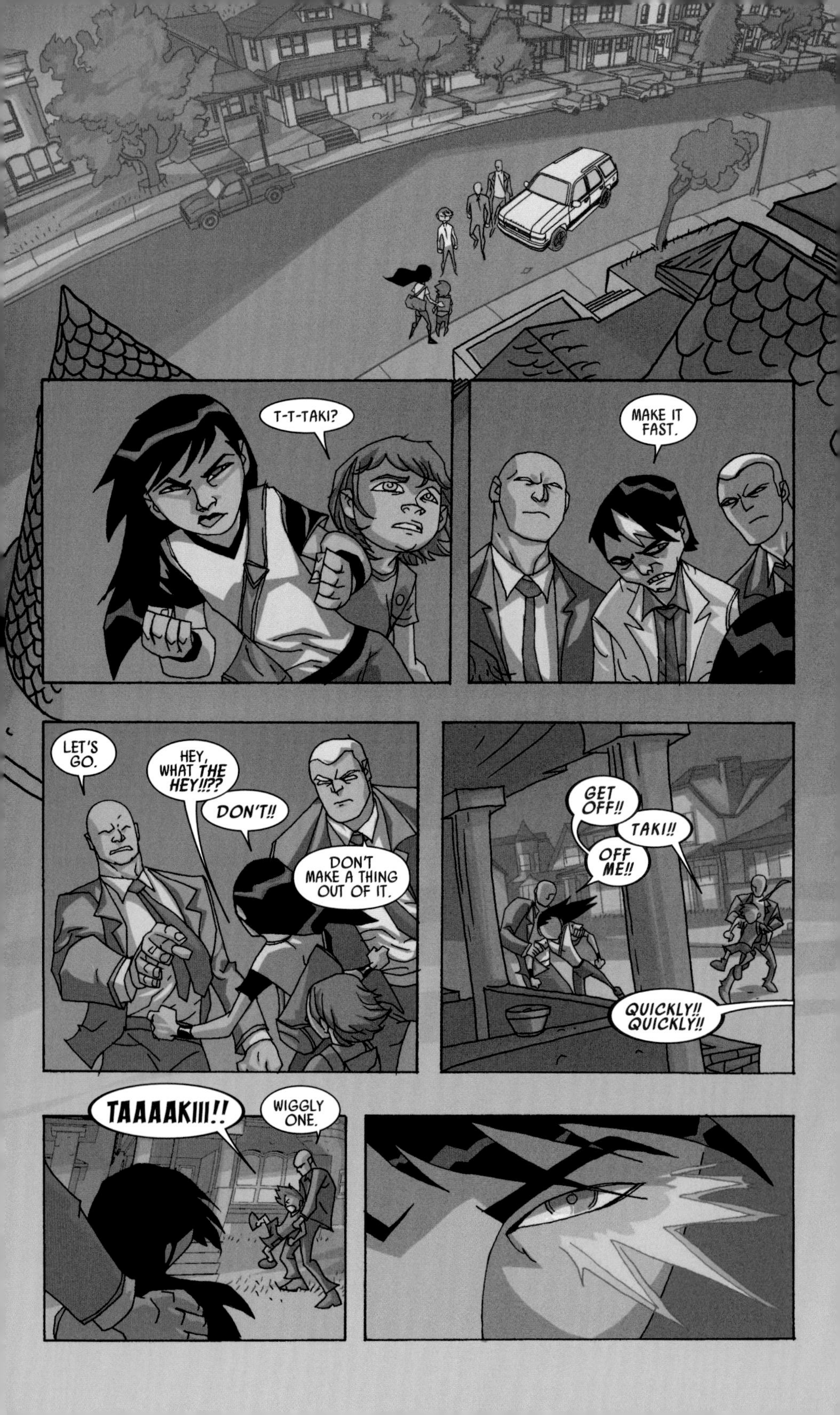
T-T-TAKI?
MAKE IT FAST.
LET'S GO.
HEY, WHAT THE HEY!!??
DON'T!!
DON'T MAKE A THING OUT OF IT.
GET OFF!!
TAKI!!
OFF ME!!
QUICKLY!! QUICKLY!!
TAAAAKIII!!
WIGGLY ONE.

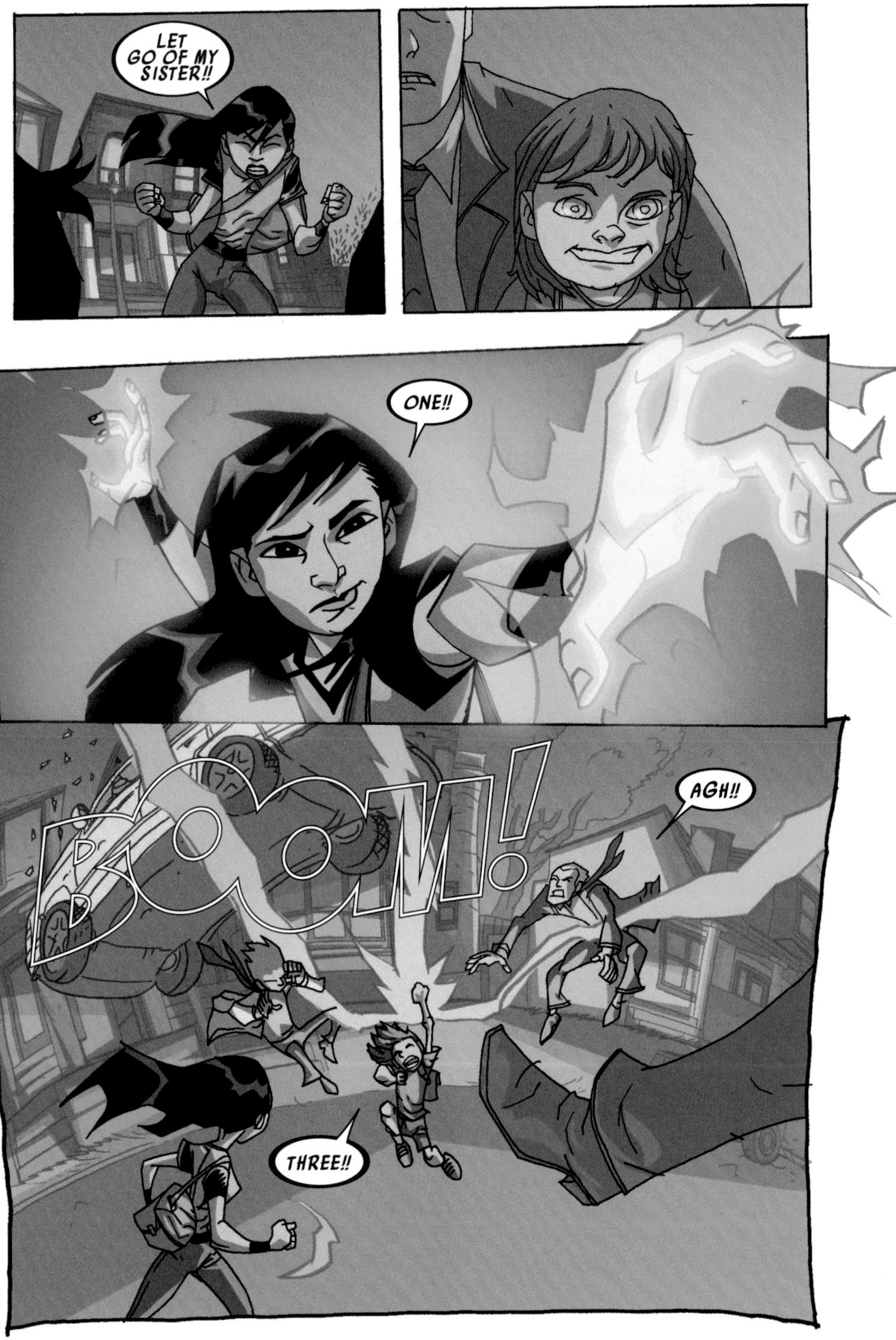

LET GO OF MY SISTER!!
ONE!!
BOOM!
AGH!!
THREE!!

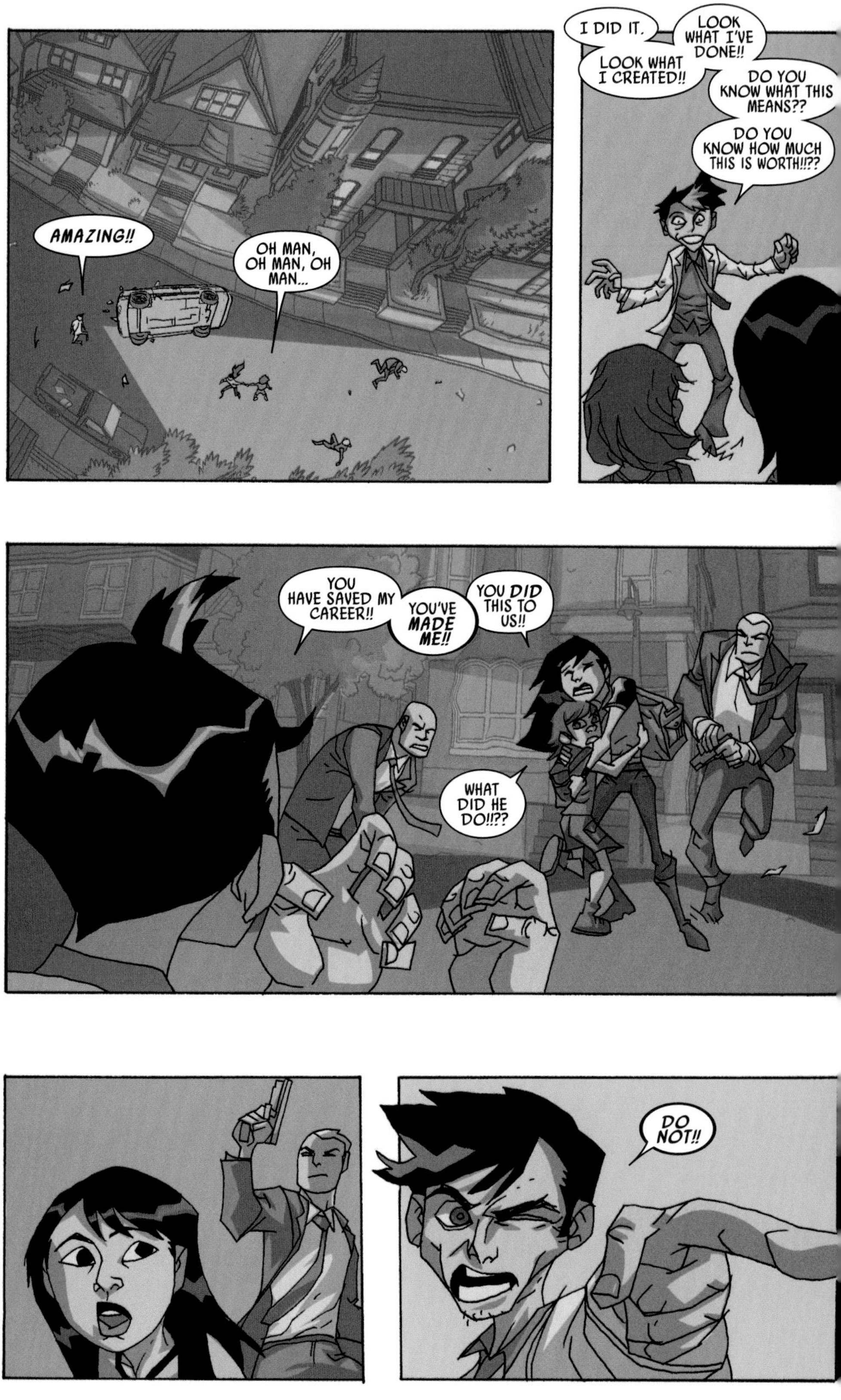
AMAZING!!
OH MAN, OH MAN, OH MAN...
I DID IT.
LOOK WHAT I'VE DONE!!
LOOK WHAT I CREATED!!
DO YOU KNOW WHAT THIS MEANS??
DO YOU KNOW HOW MUCH THIS IS WORTH!!??
YOU HAVE SAVED MY CAREER!!
YOU'VE MADE ME!!
YOU DID THIS TO US!!
WHAT DID HE DO!!??
DO NOT!!

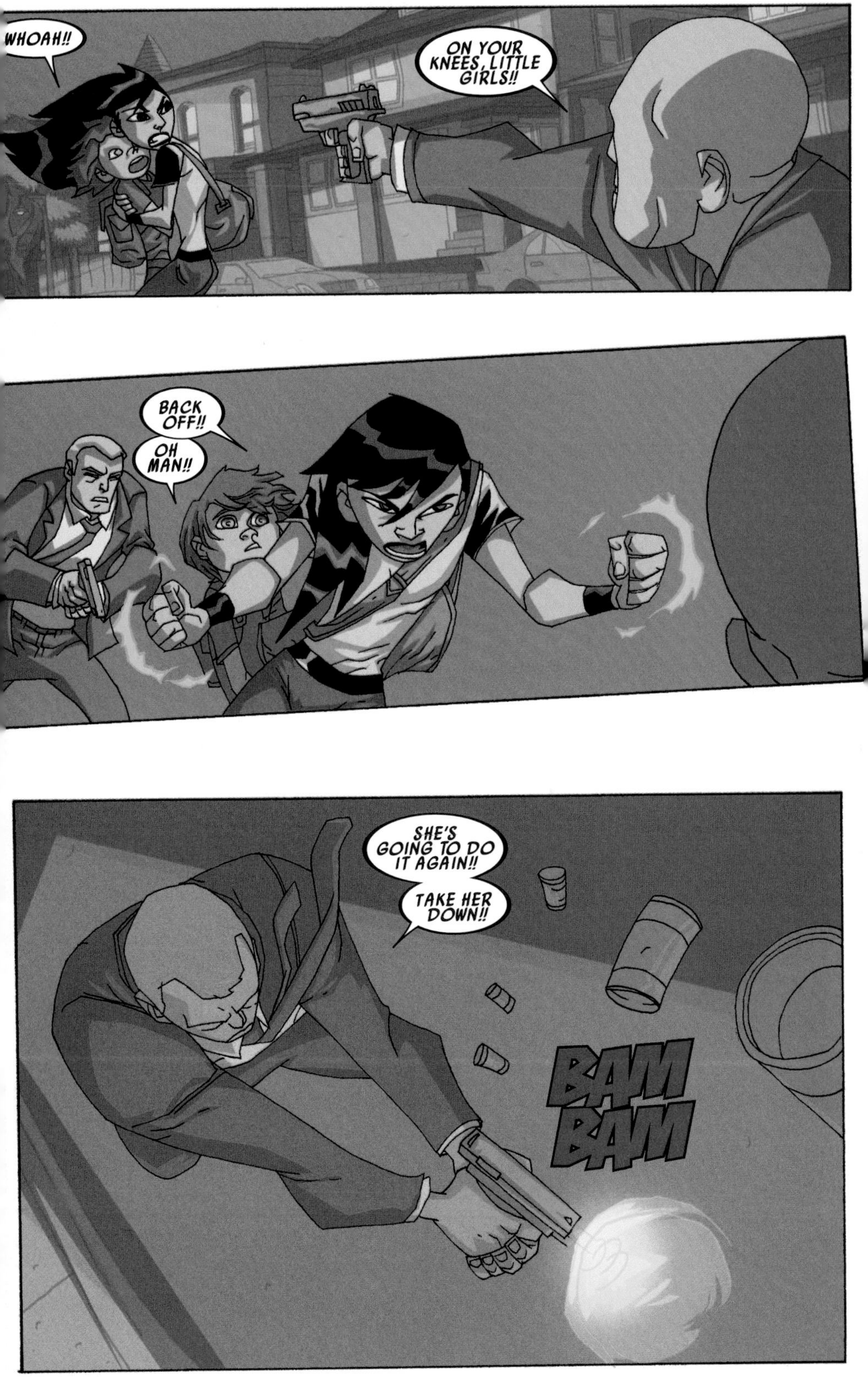
WHOAH!!
ON YOUR KNEES, LITTLE GIRLS!!
BACK OFF!!
OH MAN!!
SHE'S GOING TO DO IT AGAIN!!
TAKE HER DOWN!!
BAM BAM

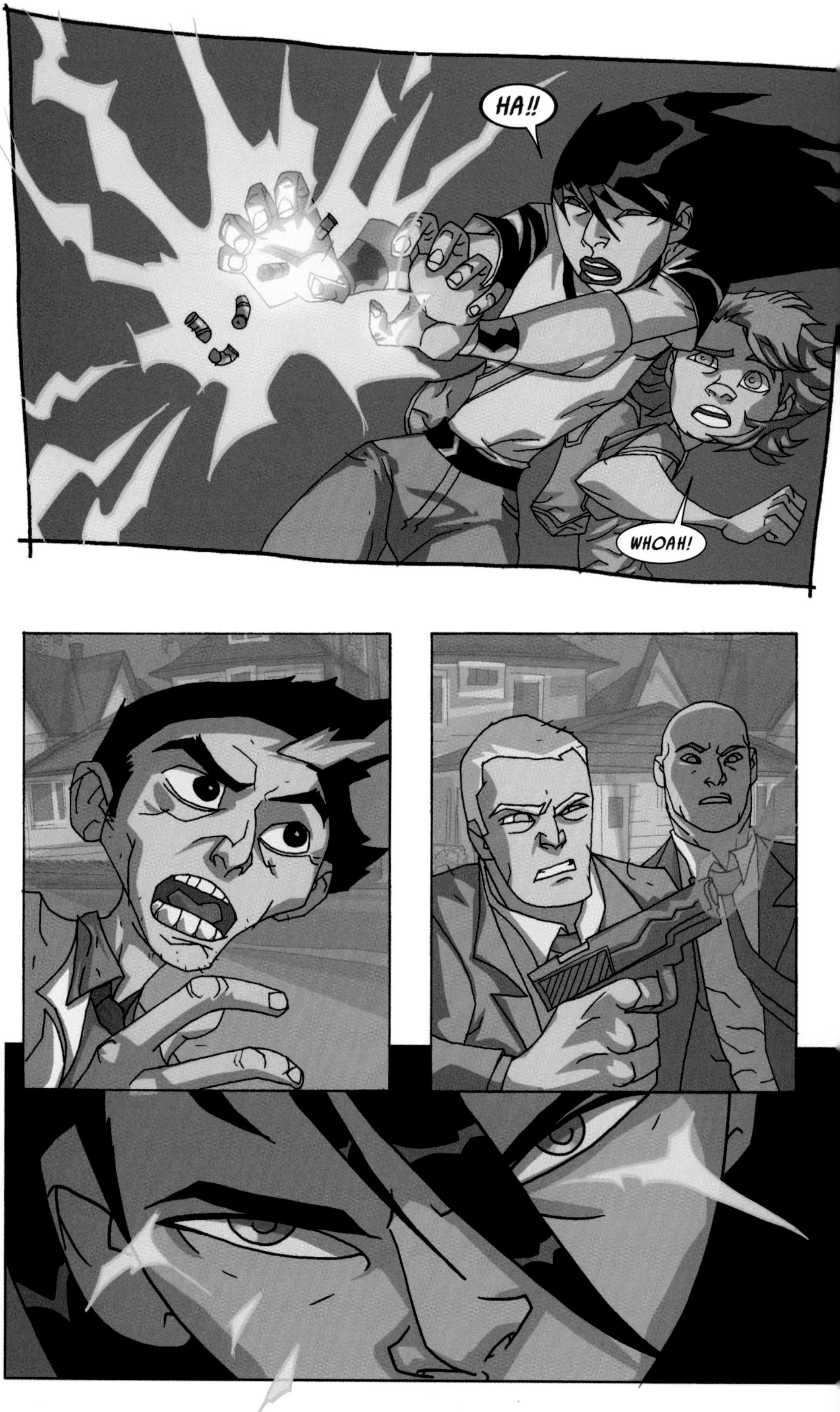
HA!!
WHOAH!

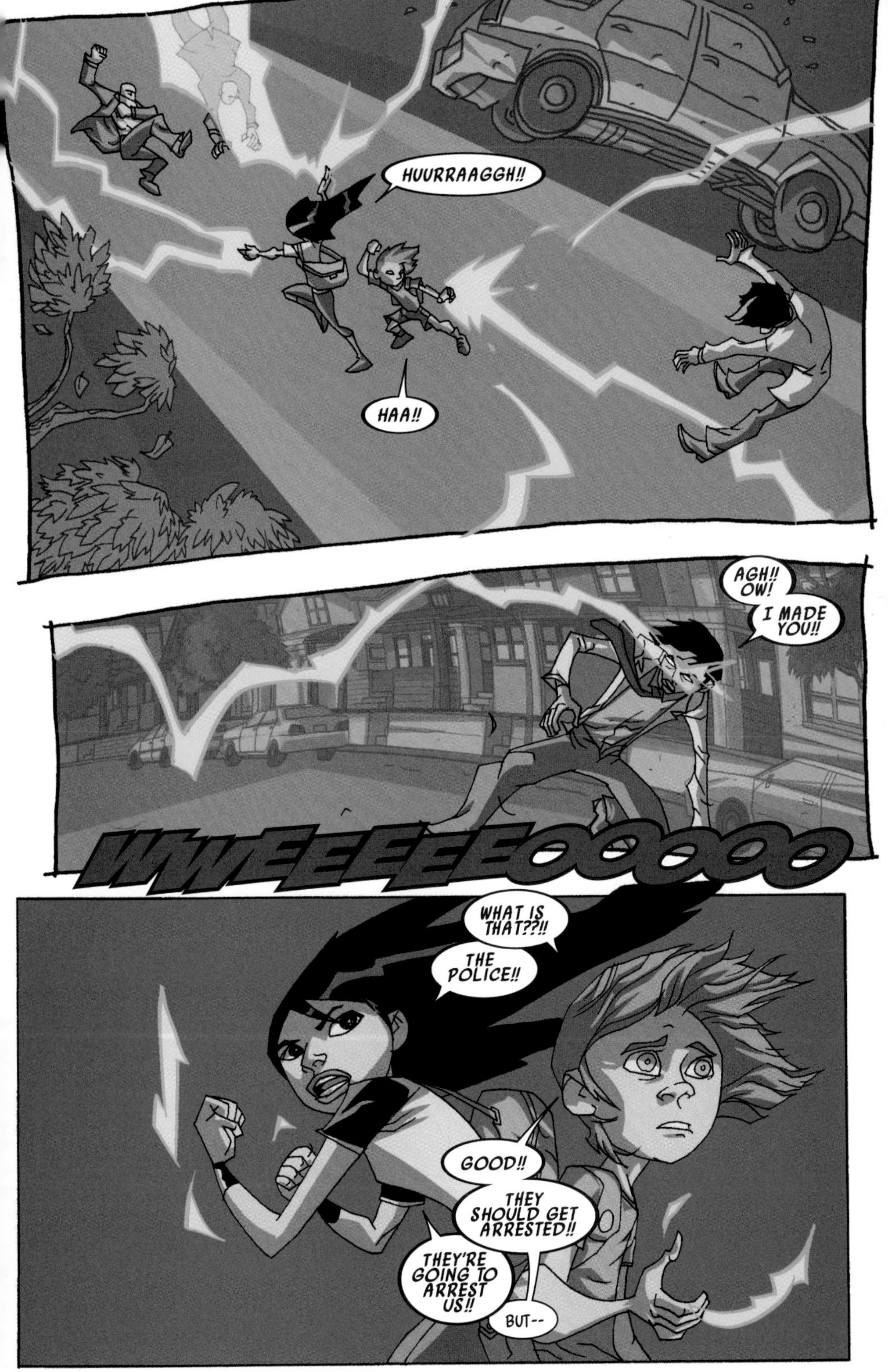
HUURRAAGGH!!
HAA!!
AGH!! OW!
I MADE YOU!!
WWEEEEEOOOOOO
WHAT IS THAT??!!
THE POLICE!!
GOOD!!
THEY SHOULD GET ARRESTED!!
THEY'RE GOING TO ARREST US!!
BUT--

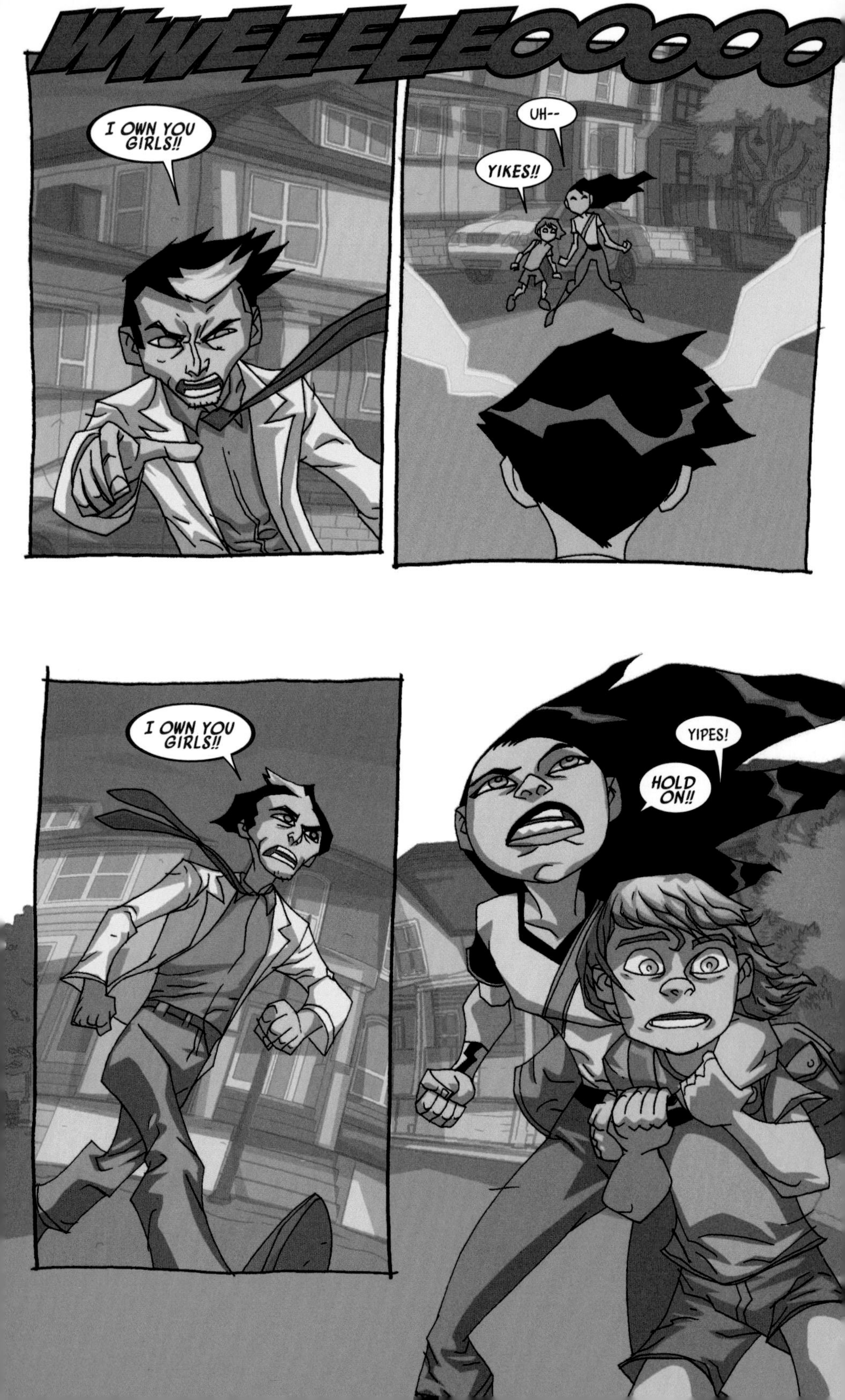
WWEEEEEOOOOOO
I OWN YOU GIRLS!!
UH--
YIKES!!
I OWN YOU GIRLS!!
YIPES!
HOLD ON!!

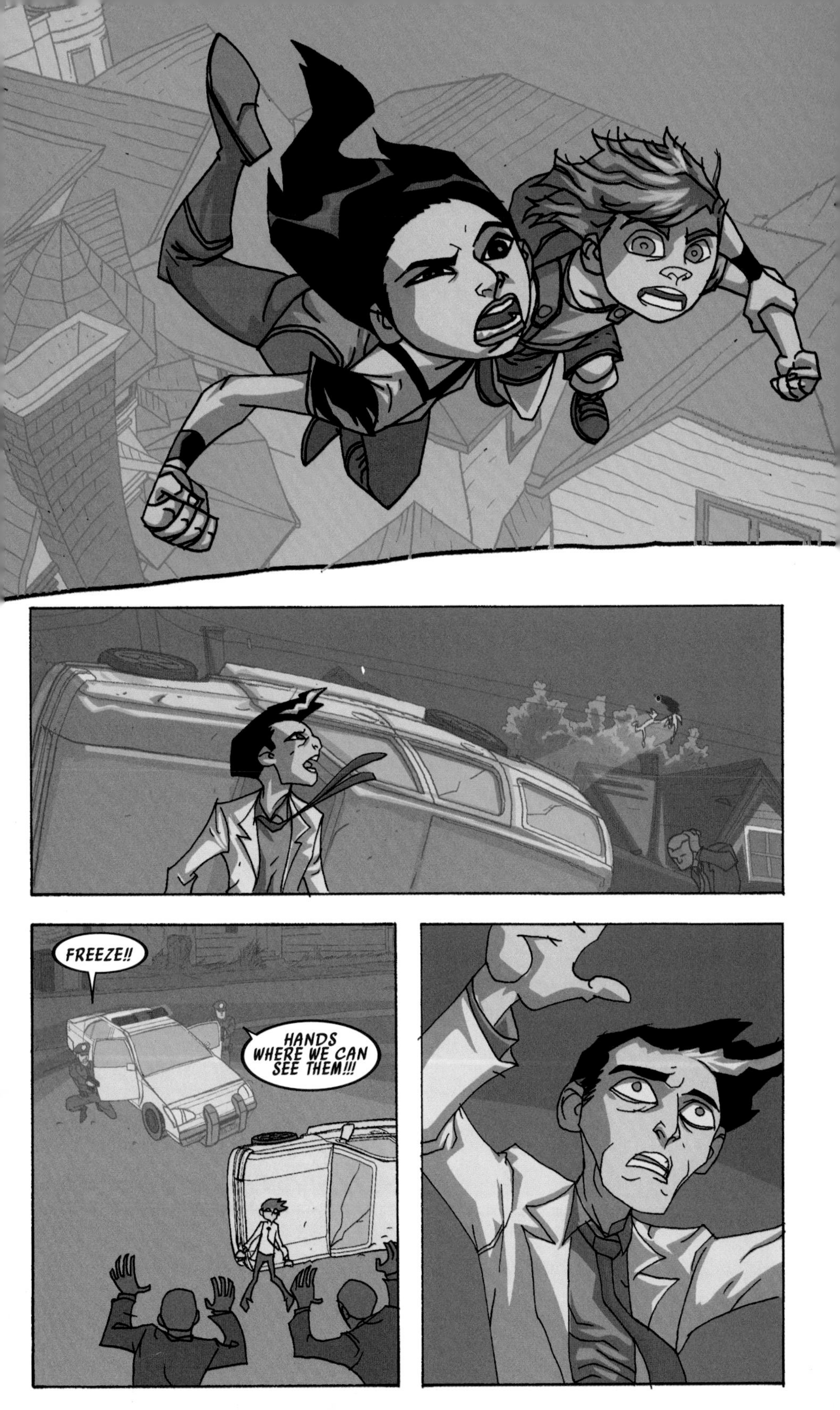
FREEZE!!
HANDS WHERE WE CAN SEE THEM!!!

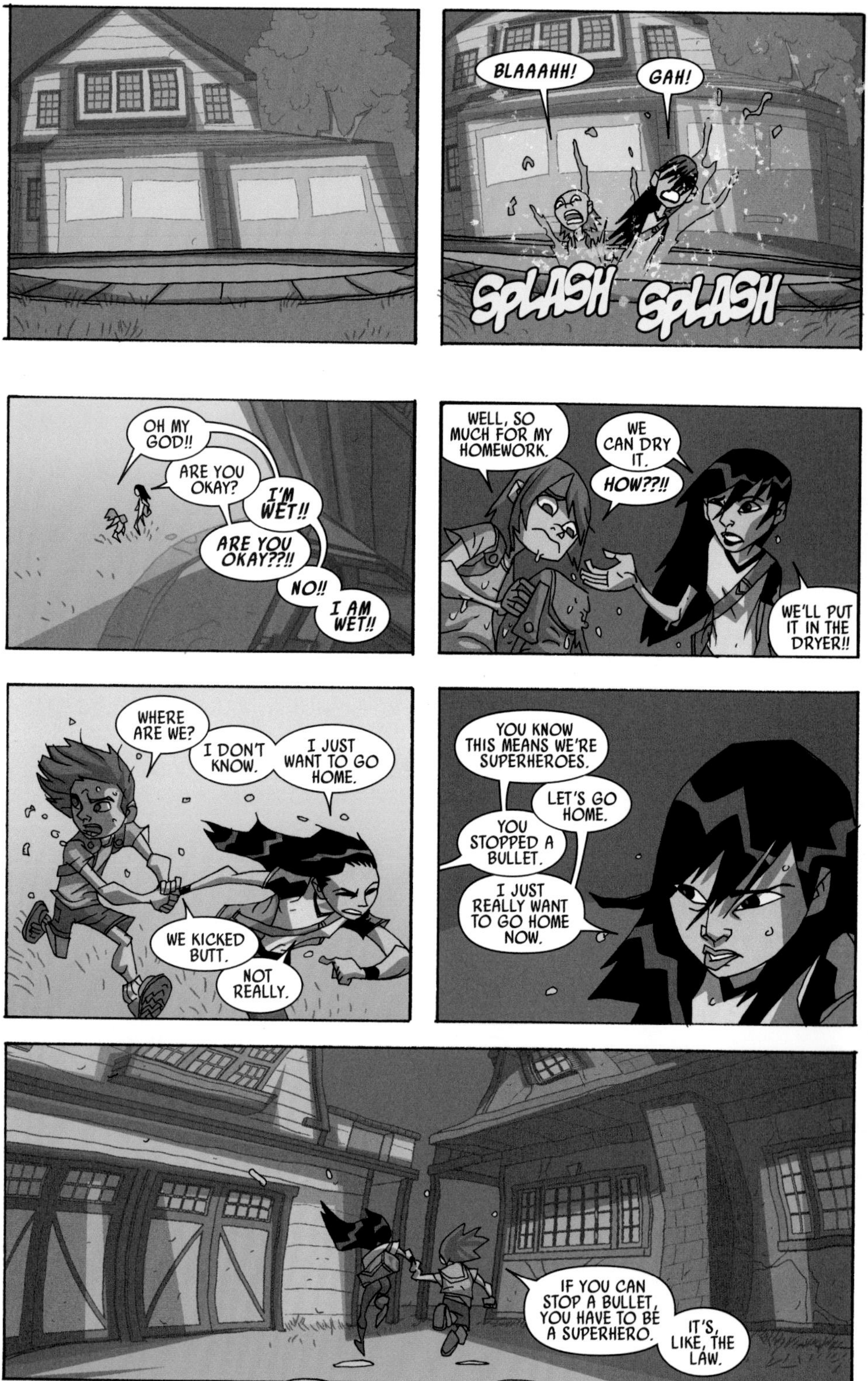
BLAAAHH!
GAH!
SPLASH SPLASH
OH MY GOD!!
ARE YOU OKAY?
I'M WET!!
ARE YOU OKAY??!!
NO!!
I AM WET!!
WELL, SO MUCH FOR MY HOMEWORK.
WE CAN DRY IT.
HOW??!!
WE'LL PUT IT IN THE DRYER!!
WHERE ARE WE?
I DON'T KNOW.
I JUST WANT TO GO HOME.
WE KICKED BUTT.
NOT REALLY.
YOU KNOW THIS MEANS WE'RE SUPERHEROES.
LET'S GO HOME.
YOU STOPPED A BULLET.
I JUST REALLY WANT TO GO HOME NOW.
IF YOU CAN STOP A BULLET, YOU HAVE TO BE A SUPERHERO.
IT'S, LIKE, THE LAW.

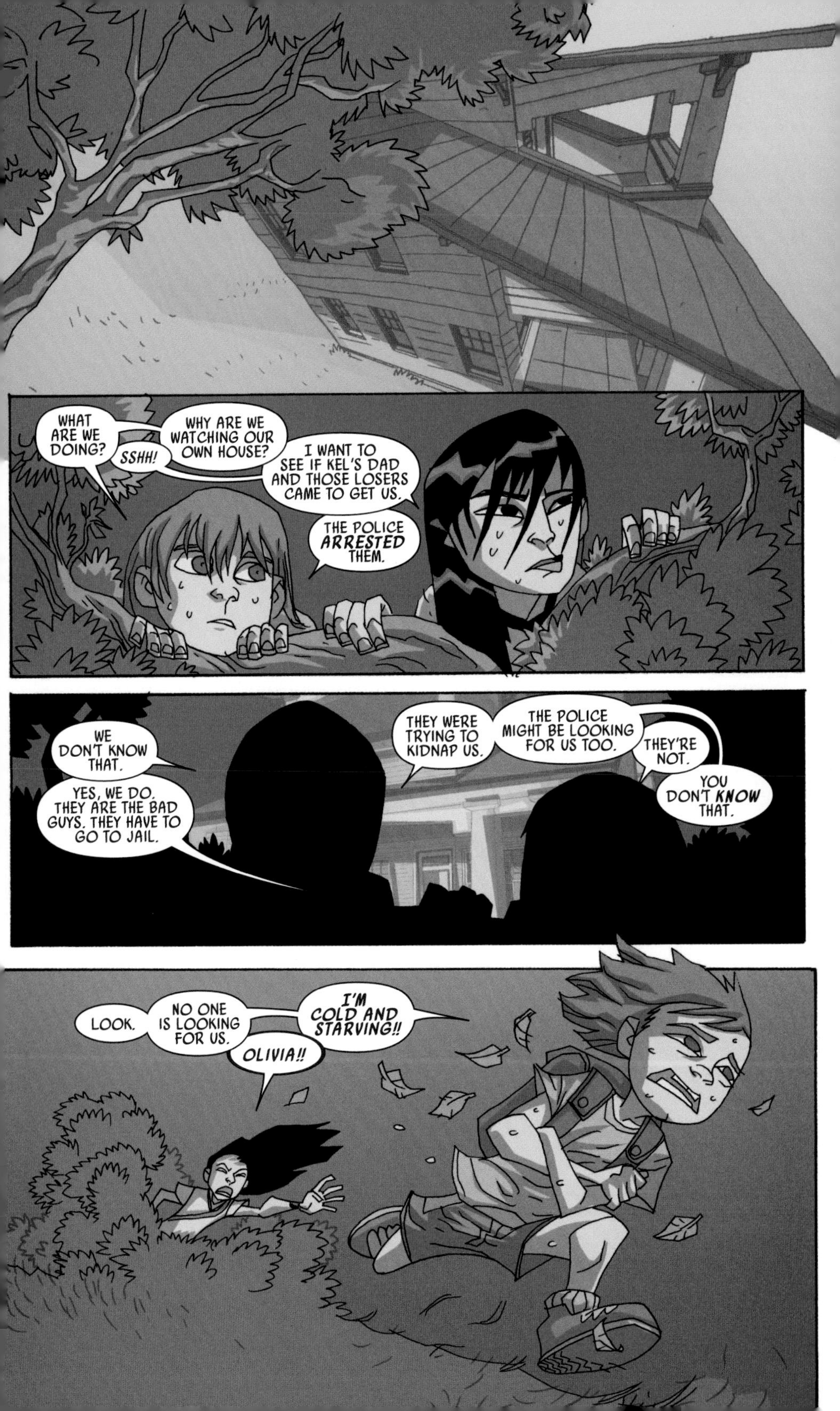
WHAT ARE WE DOING?
WHY ARE WE WATCHING OUR OWN HOUSE?
SSHH!
I WANT TO SEE IF KEL'S DAD AND THOSE LOSERS CAME TO GET US.
THE POLICE ARRESTED THEM.
WE DON'T KNOW THAT.
YES, WE DO. THEY ARE THE BAD GUYS. THEY HAVE TO GO TO JAIL.
THEY WERE TRYING TO KIDNAP US.
THE POLICE MIGHT BE LOOKING FOR US TOO.
THEY'RE NOT.
YOU DON'T KNOW THAT.
LOOK.
NO ONE IS LOOKING FOR US.
I'M COLD AND STARVING!!
OLIVIA!!

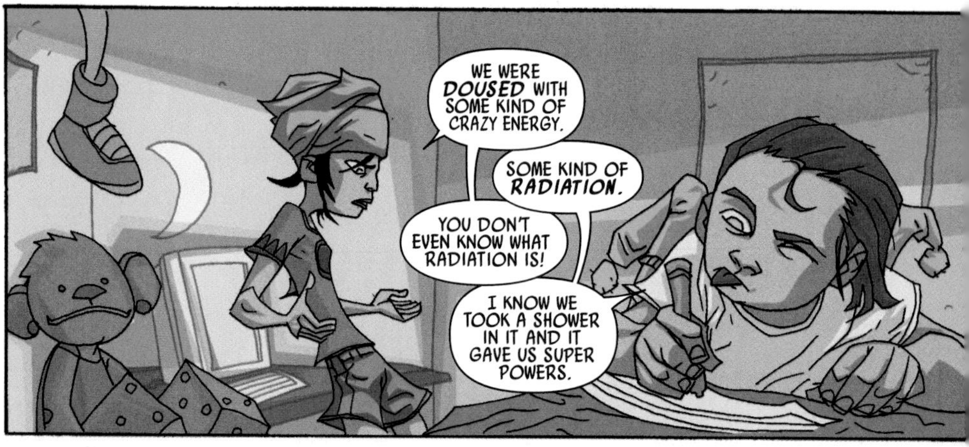
WE WERE DOUSED WITH SOME KIND OF CRAZY ENERGY.
SOME KIND OF RADIATION.
YOU DON'T EVEN KNOW WHAT RADIATION IS!
I KNOW WE TOOK A SHOWER IN IT AND IT GAVE US SUPER POWERS.

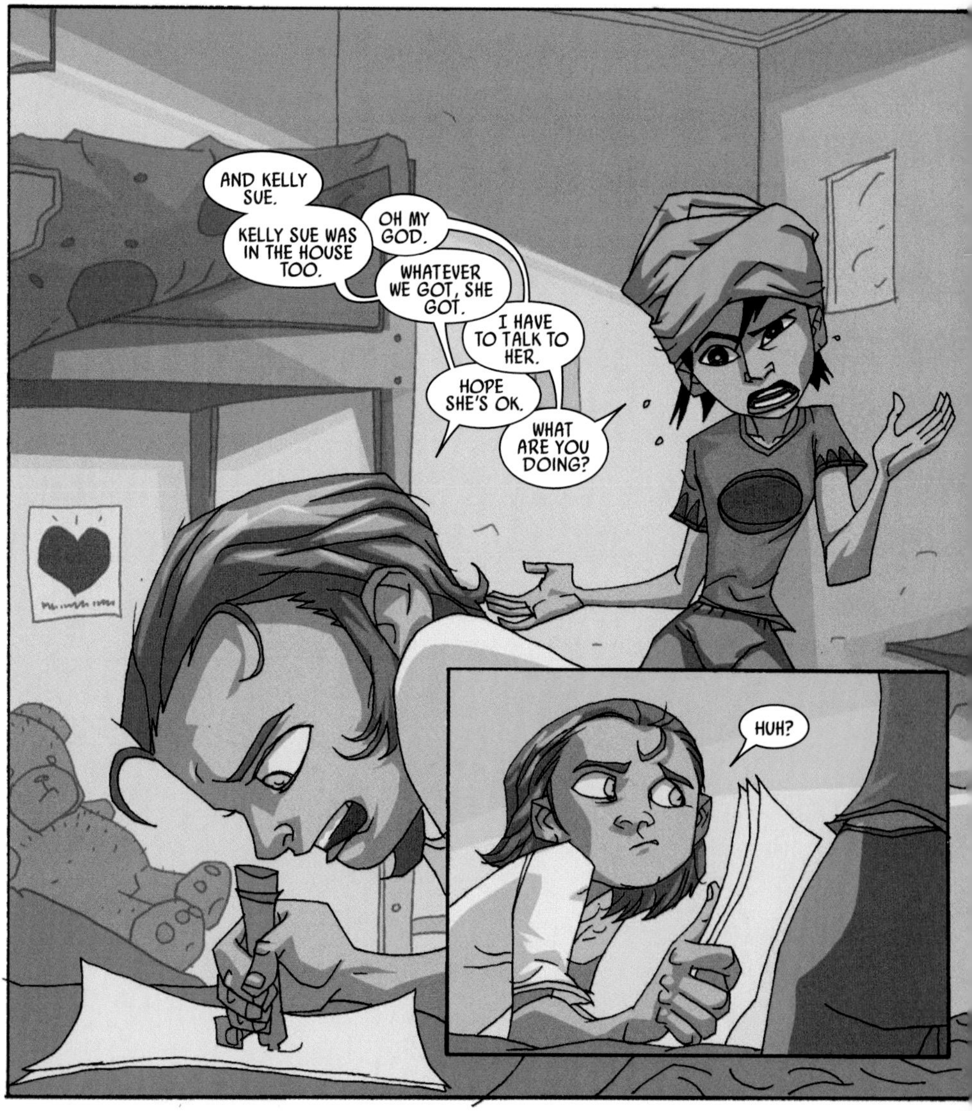
AND KELLY SUE.
KELLY SUE WAS IN THE HOUSE TOO.
OH MY GOD.
WHATEVER WE GOT, SHE GOT.
I HAVE TO TALK TO HER.
HOPE SHE'S OK.
WHAT ARE YOU DOING?
HUH?

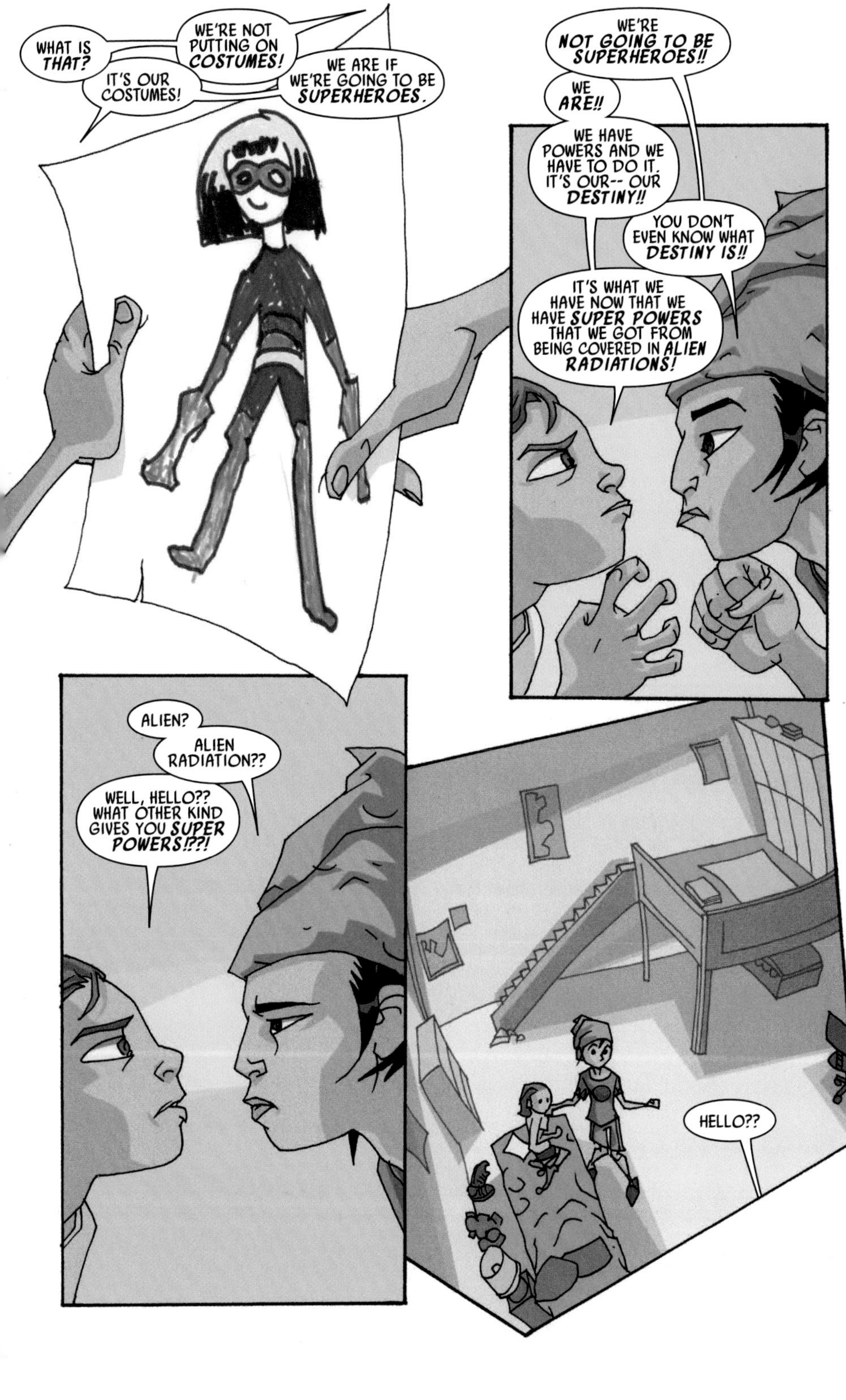

WHAT IS THAT?
IT'S OUR COSTUMES!
WE'RE NOT PUTTING ON COSTUMES!
WE ARE IF WE'RE GOING TO BE SUPERHEROES.
WE'RE NOT GOING TO BE SUPERHEROES!!
WE ARE!!
WE HAVE POWERS AND WE HAVE TO DO IT. IT'S OUR-- OUR DESTINY!!
YOU DON'T EVEN KNOW WHAT DESTINY IS!!
IT'S WHAT WE HAVE NOW THAT WE HAVE SUPER POWERS THAT WE GOT FROM BEING COVERED IN ALIEN RADIATIONS!
ALIEN?
ALIEN RADIATION??
WELL, HELLO?? WHAT OTHER KIND GIVES YOU SUPER POWERS!??!
HELLO??

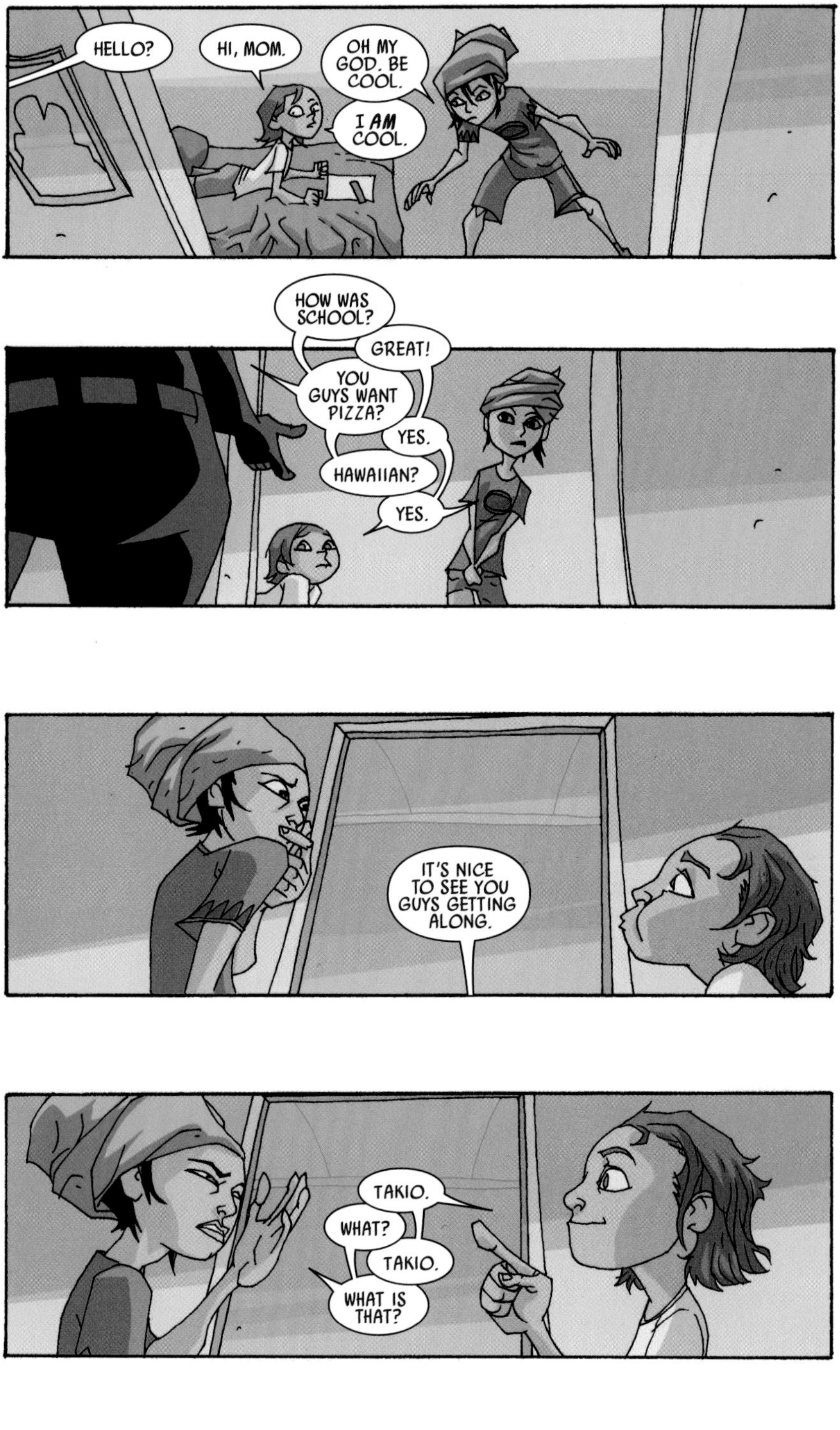
HELLO?
HI, MOM.
OH MY GOD. BE COOL.
I *AM* COOL.
HOW WAS SCHOOL?
GREAT!
YOU GUYS WANT PIZZA?
YES.
HAWAIIAN?
YES.
IT'S NICE TO SEE YOU GUYS GETTING ALONG.
TAKIO.
WHAT?
TAKIO.
WHAT IS THAT?

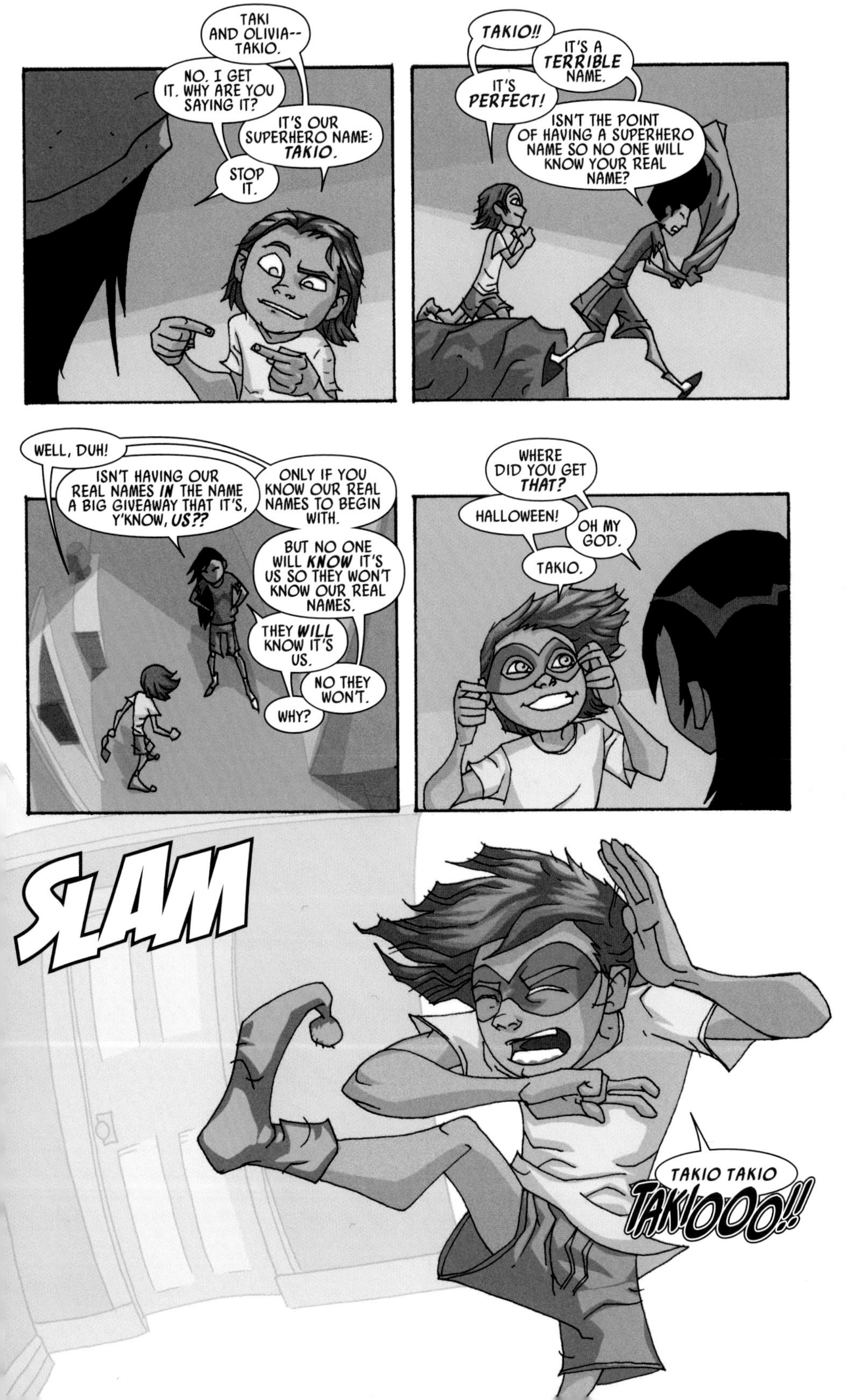
TAKI AND OLIVIA-- TAKIO.
NO. I GET IT. WHY ARE YOU SAYING IT?
IT'S OUR SUPERHERO NAME: TAKIO.
STOP IT.
TAKIO!!
IT'S A TERRIBLE NAME.
IT'S PERFECT!
ISN'T THE POINT OF HAVING A SUPERHERO NAME SO NO ONE WILL KNOW YOUR REAL NAME?
WELL, DUH!
ISN'T HAVING OUR REAL NAMES IN THE NAME A BIG GIVEAWAY THAT IT'S, Y'KNOW, US??
ONLY IF YOU KNOW OUR REAL NAMES TO BEGIN WITH.
BUT NO ONE WILL KNOW IT'S US SO THEY WON'T KNOW OUR REAL NAMES.
THEY WILL KNOW IT'S US.
NO THEY WON'T.
WHY?
WHERE DID YOU GET THAT?
HALLOWEEN!
OH MY GOD.
TAKIO.
SLAM
TAKIO TAKIO
TAKIOOO!!

SMASSHHH

VRRRROOM

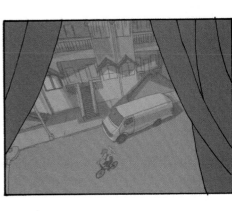

PORTLAND NEWS

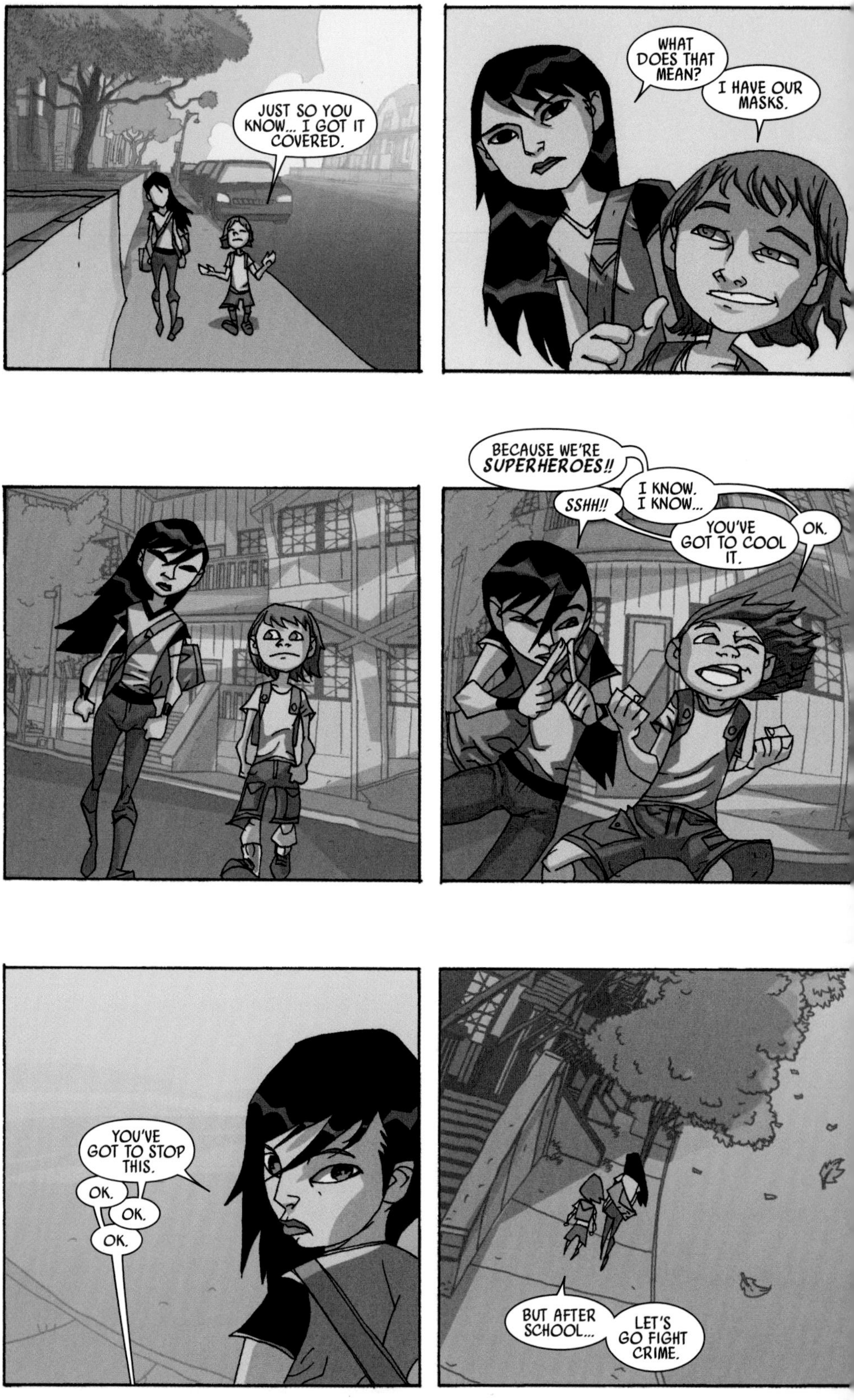
JUST SO YOU KNOW... I GOT IT COVERED.
WHAT DOES THAT MEAN?
I HAVE OUR MASKS.
BECAUSE WE'RE SUPERHEROES!!
SSHH!!
I KNOW. I KNOW...
YOU'VE GOT TO COOL IT.
OK.
YOU'VE GOT TO STOP THIS.
OK.
OK.
OK.
BUT AFTER SCHOOL...
LET'S GO FIGHT CRIME.

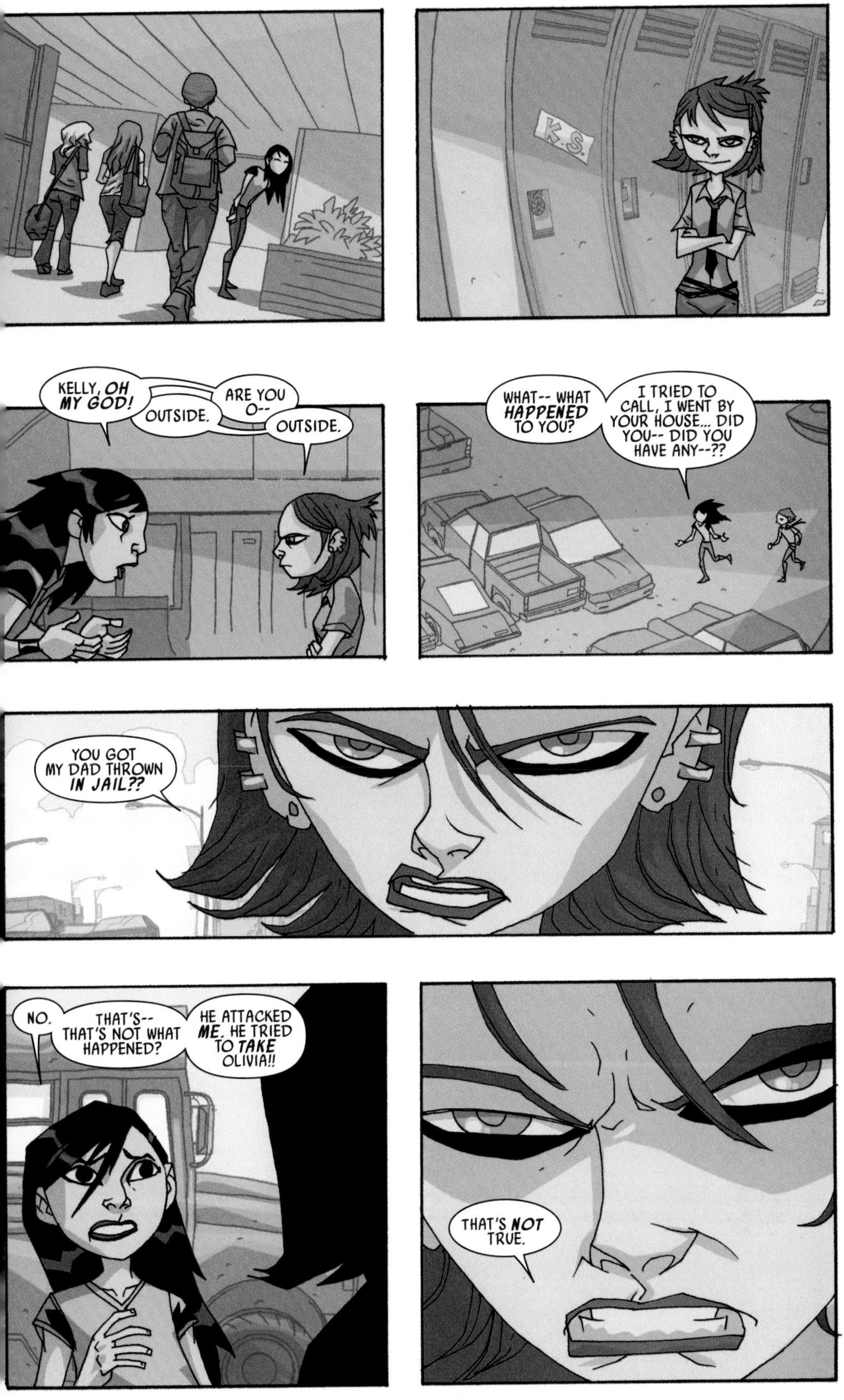
KELLY, OH MY GOD!
OUTSIDE.
ARE YOU O--
OUTSIDE.
WHAT-- WHAT HAPPENED TO YOU?
I TRIED TO CALL, I WENT BY YOUR HOUSE... DID YOU-- DID YOU HAVE ANY--??
YOU GOT MY DAD THROWN IN JAIL??
NO.
THAT'S-- THAT'S NOT WHAT HAPPENED?
HE ATTACKED ME. HE TRIED TO TAKE OLIVIA!!
THAT'S NOT TRUE.

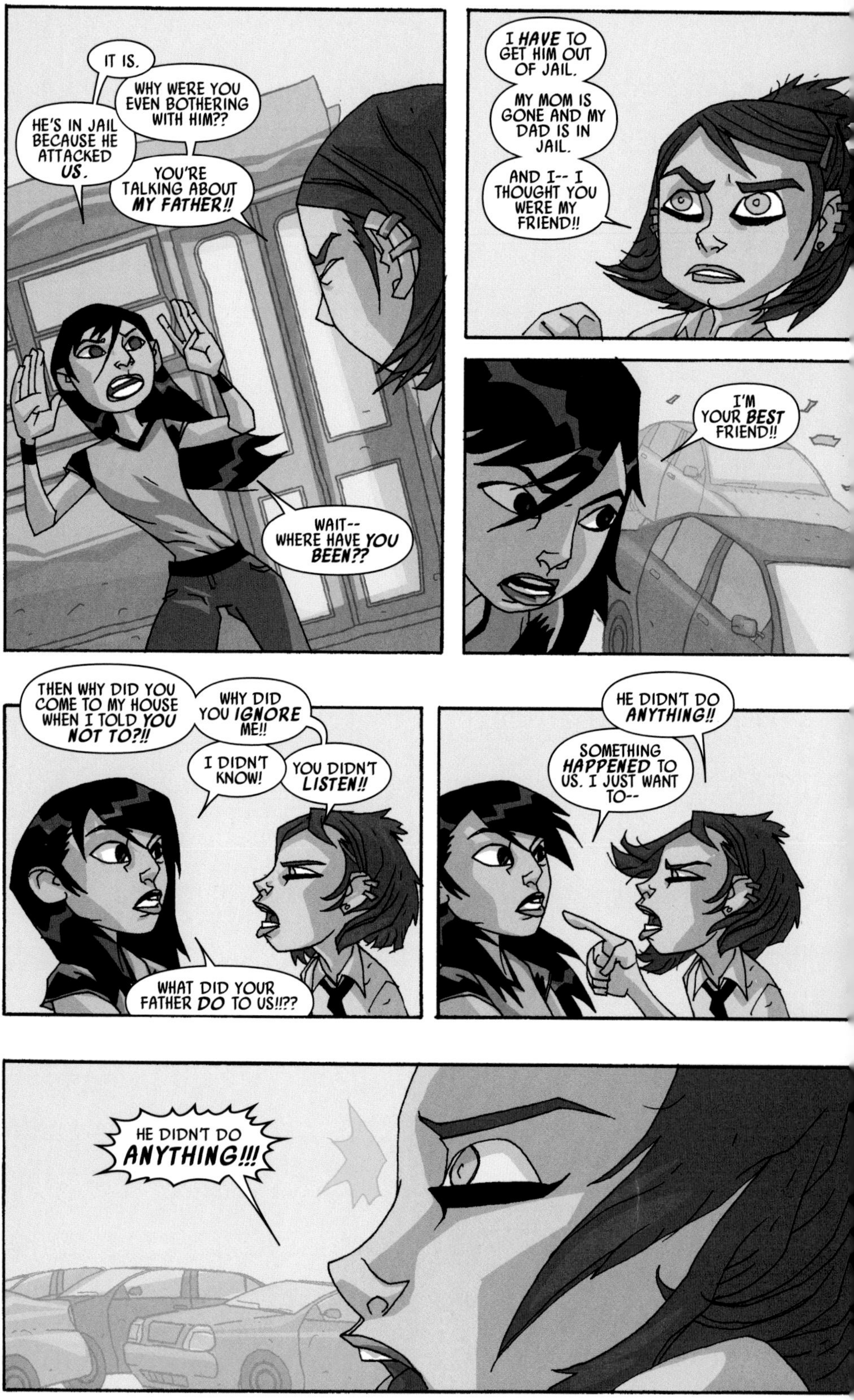
IT IS.
HE'S IN JAIL BECAUSE HE ATTACKED *US.*
WHY WERE YOU EVEN BOTHERING WITH HIM??
YOU'RE TALKING ABOUT *MY FATHER!!*
WAIT-- WHERE HAVE *YOU BEEN??*
I *HAVE* TO GET HIM OUT OF JAIL.
MY MOM IS GONE AND MY DAD IS IN JAIL.
AND I-- I THOUGHT YOU WERE MY FRIEND!!
I'M YOUR *BEST* FRIEND!!
THEN WHY DID YOU COME TO MY HOUSE WHEN I TOLD *YOU NOT TO?!!*
WHY DID YOU *IGNORE* ME!!
I DIDN'T KNOW!
YOU DIDN'T *LISTEN!!*
WHAT DID YOUR FATHER *DO* TO US!!??
HE DIDN'T DO *ANYTHING!!*
SOMETHING *HAPPENED* TO US. I JUST WANT TO--
HE DIDN'T DO *ANYTHING!!!*

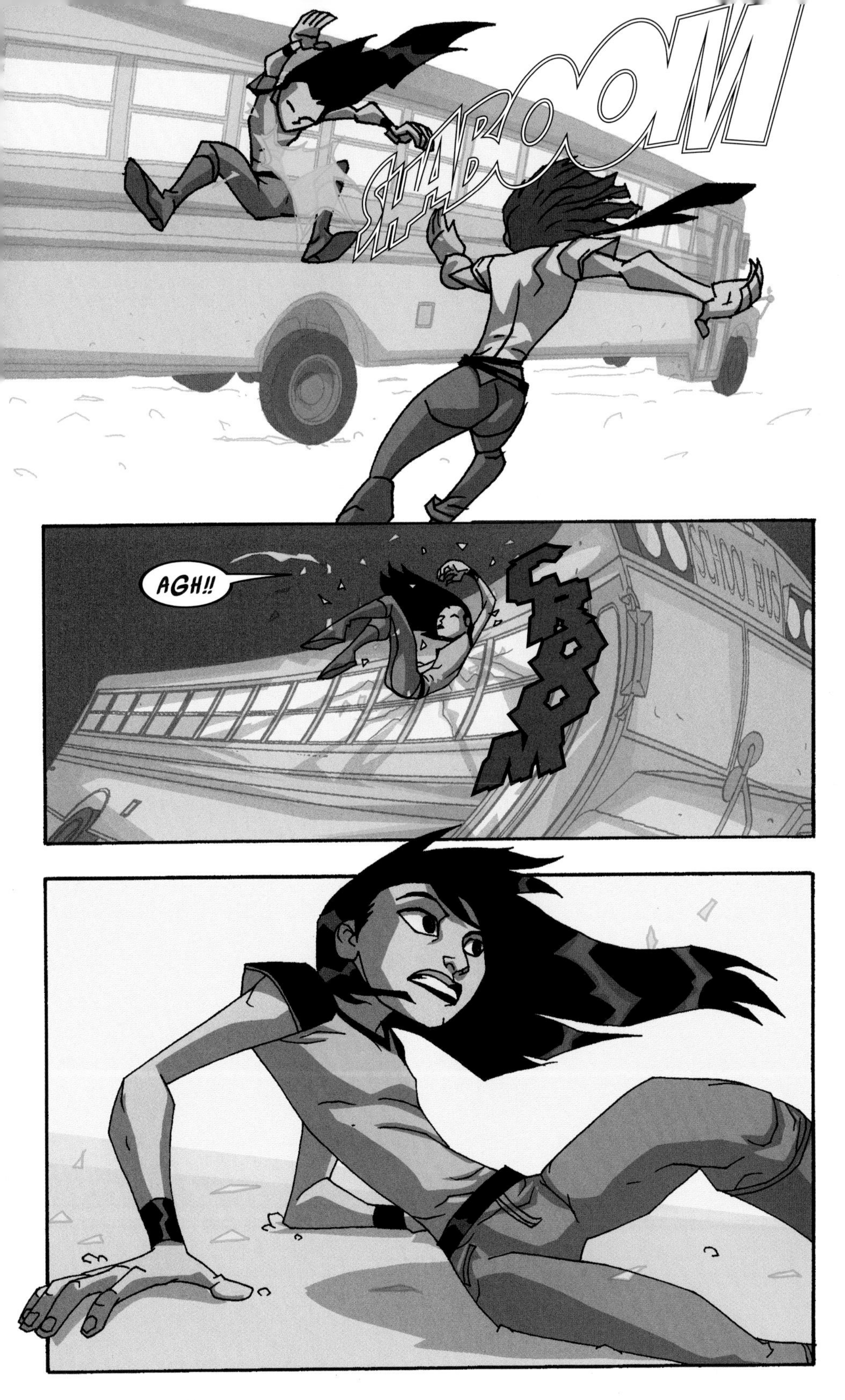
SHABOOM
AGH!!
CROOM
SCHOOL BUS

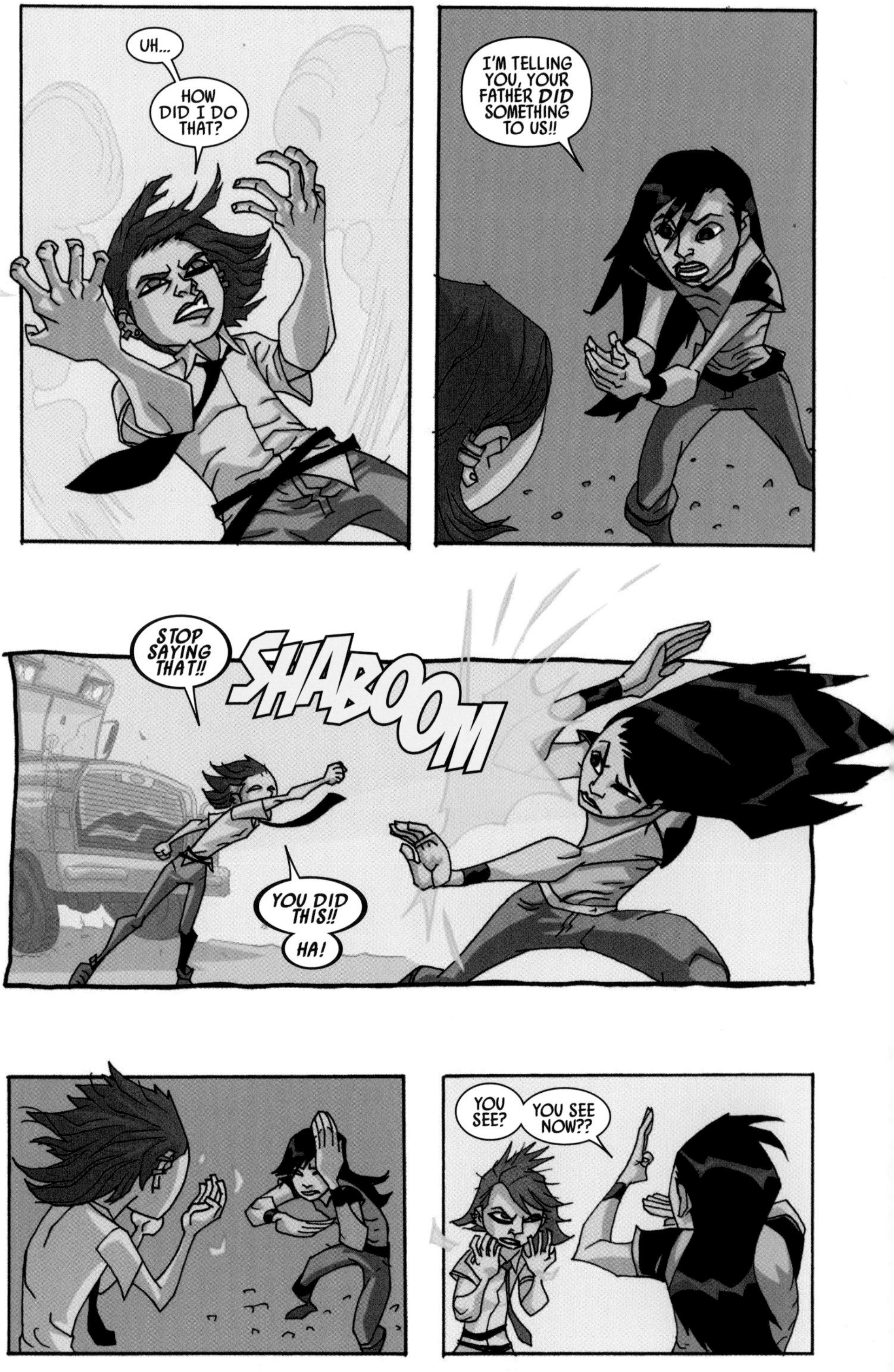
UH...
HOW DID I DO THAT?
I'M TELLING YOU, YOUR FATHER DID SOMETHING TO US!!
STOP SAYING THAT!!
SHABOOM
YOU DID THIS!!
HA!
YOU SEE?
YOU SEE NOW??

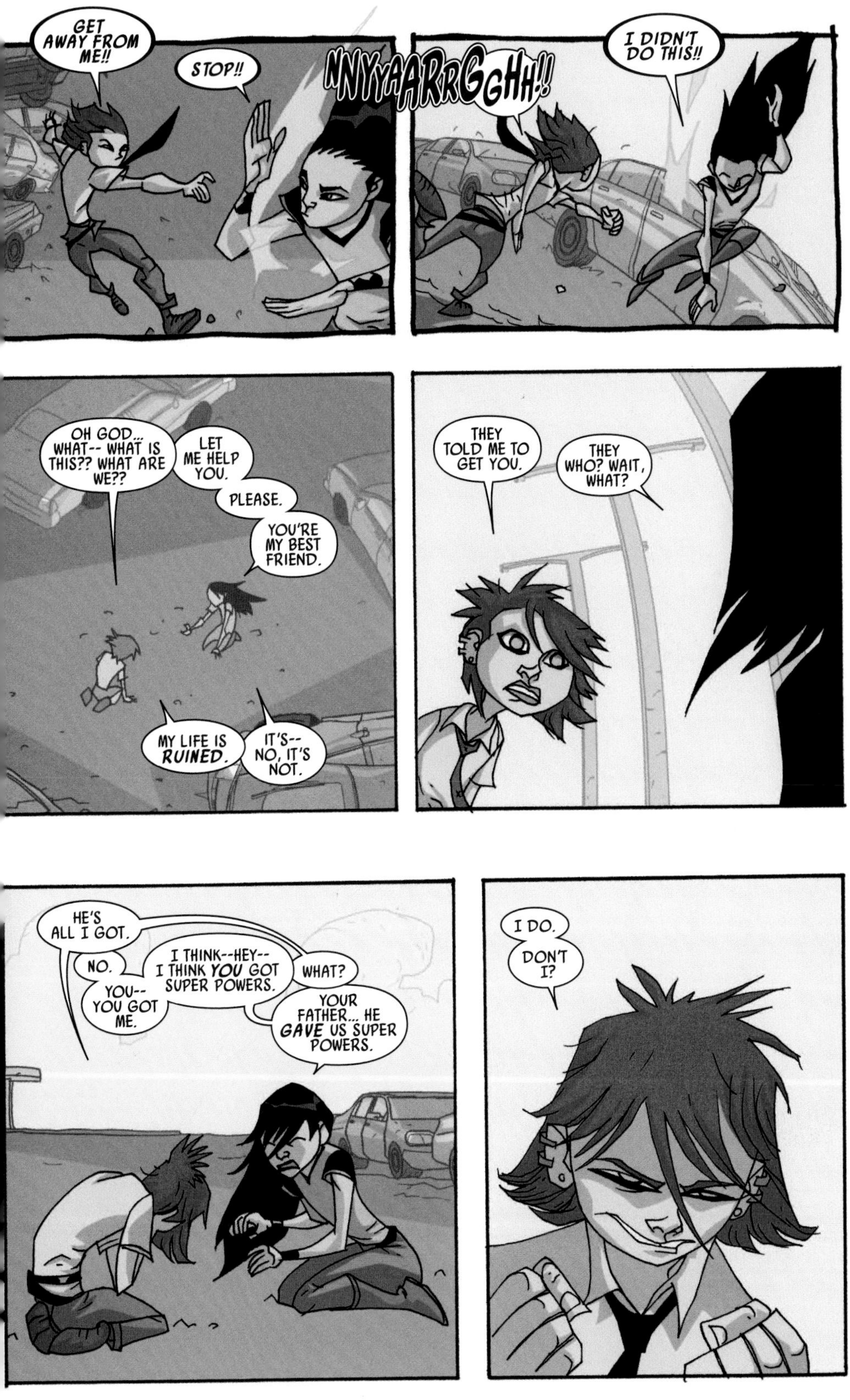
GET AWAY FROM ME!!
STOP!!
NNYYAARRGGHH!!
I DIDN'T DO THIS!!
OH GOD... WHAT-- WHAT IS THIS?? WHAT ARE WE??
LET ME HELP YOU.
PLEASE.
YOU'RE MY BEST FRIEND.
MY LIFE IS RUINED.
IT'S-- NO, IT'S NOT.
THEY TOLD ME TO GET YOU.
THEY WHO? WAIT, WHAT?
HE'S ALL I GOT.
NO.
YOU-- YOU GOT ME.
I THINK--HEY-- I THINK YOU GOT SUPER POWERS.
WHAT?
YOUR FATHER... HE GAVE US SUPER POWERS.
I DO.
DON'T I?

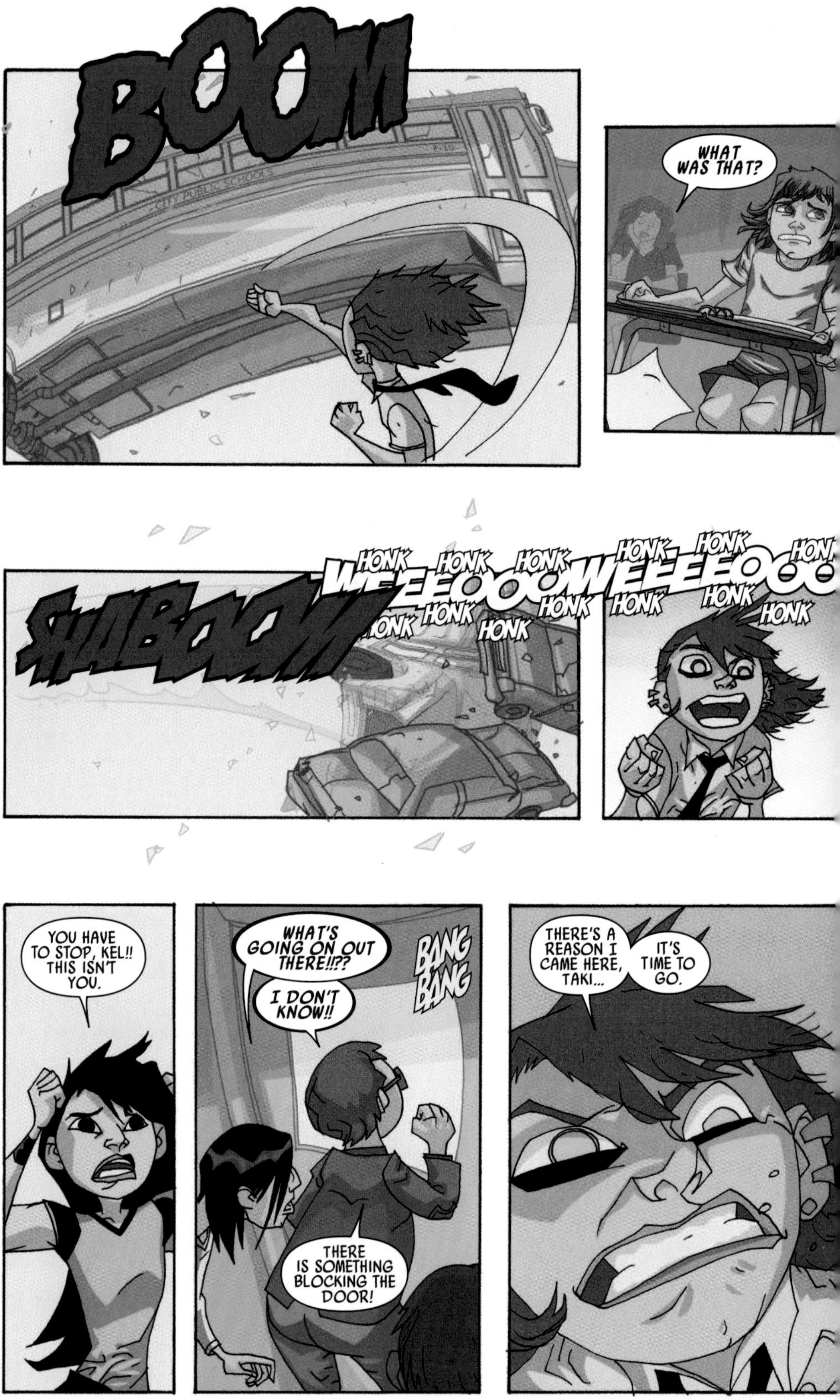
BOOM
WHAT WAS THAT?
SHABOOM
HONK HONK HONK HONK HONK HONK
WEEEOOOOWEEEEOOO
HONK HONK HONK HONK HONK HONK HONK
YOU HAVE TO STOP, KEL!! THIS ISN'T YOU.
WHAT'S GOING ON OUT THERE!!??
I DON'T KNOW!!
BANG BANG
THERE IS SOMETHING BLOCKING THE DOOR!
THERE'S A REASON I CAME HERE, TAKI...
IT'S TIME TO GO.

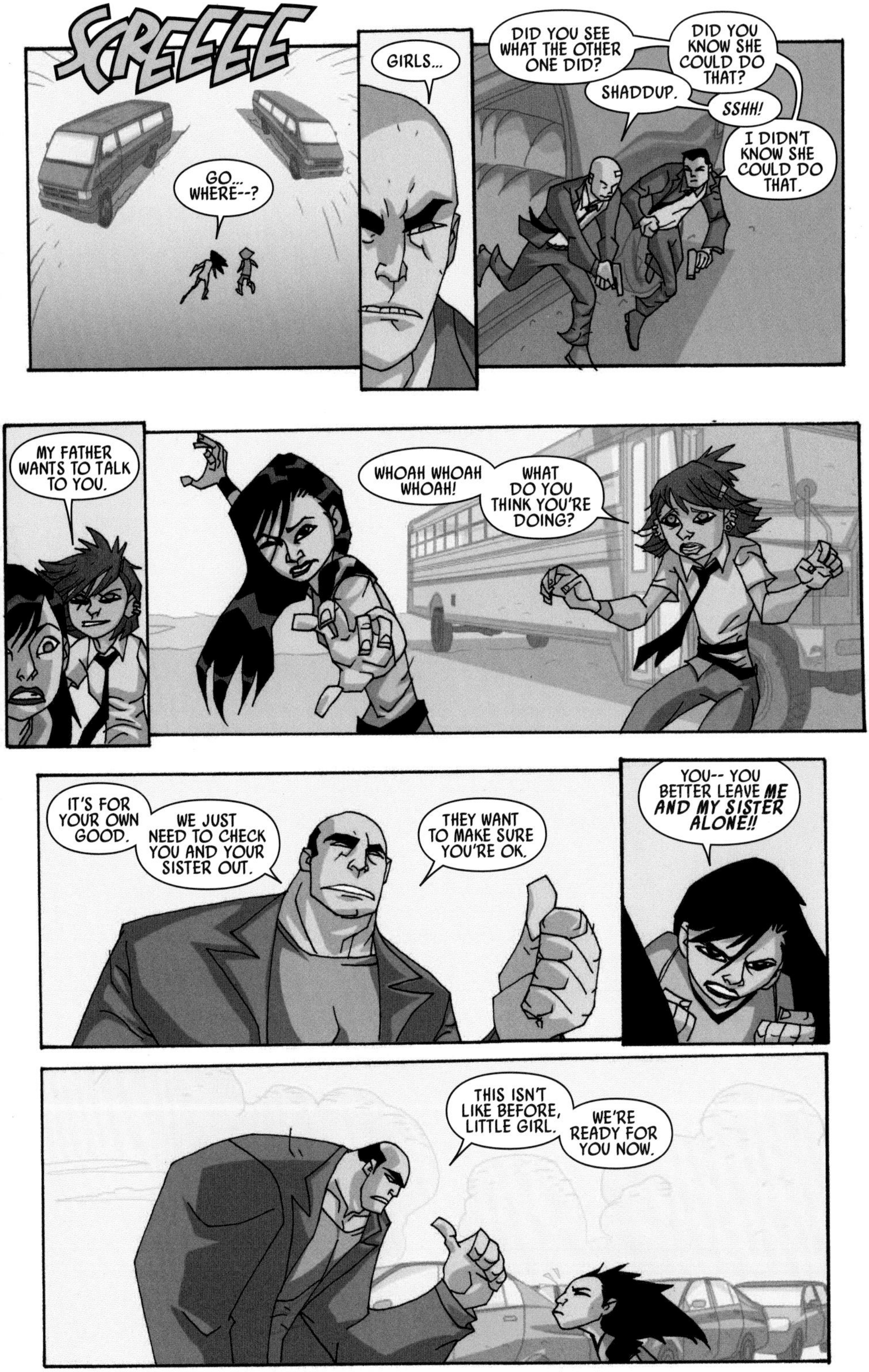
SCREEEE
GO... WHERE--?
GIRLS...
DID YOU SEE WHAT THE OTHER ONE DID?
DID YOU KNOW SHE COULD DO THAT?
SHADDUP.
SSHH!
I DIDN'T KNOW SHE COULD DO THAT.
MY FATHER WANTS TO TALK TO YOU.
WHOAH WHOAH WHOAH!
WHAT DO YOU THINK YOU'RE DOING?
IT'S FOR YOUR OWN GOOD.
WE JUST NEED TO CHECK YOU AND YOUR SISTER OUT.
THEY WANT TO MAKE SURE YOU'RE OK.
YOU-- YOU BETTER LEAVE ME AND MY SISTER ALONE!!
THIS ISN'T LIKE BEFORE, LITTLE GIRL.
WE'RE READY FOR YOU NOW.

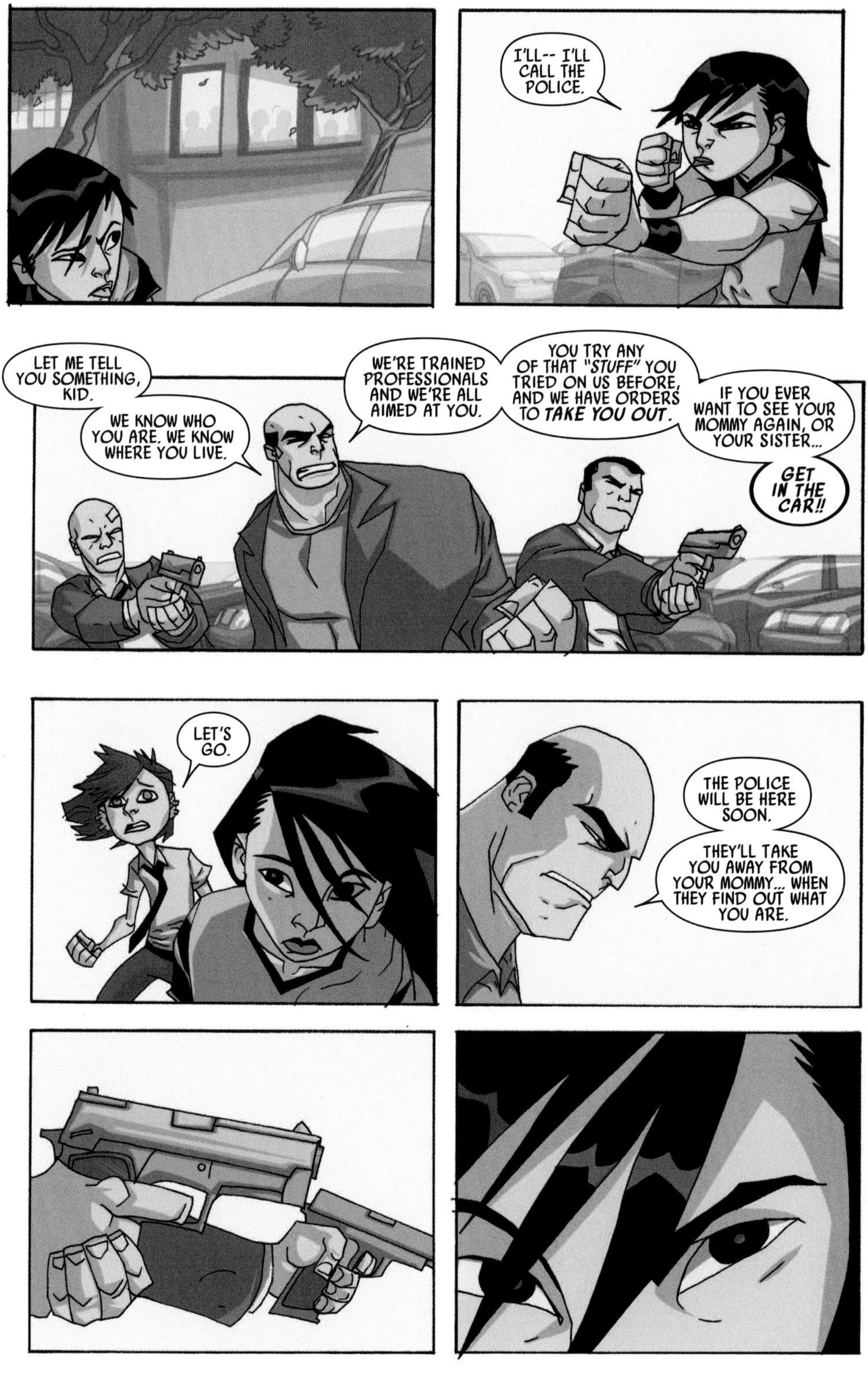
I'LL-- I'LL CALL THE POLICE.
LET ME TELL YOU SOMETHING, KID.
WE KNOW WHO YOU ARE. WE KNOW WHERE YOU LIVE.
WE'RE TRAINED PROFESSIONALS AND WE'RE ALL AIMED AT YOU.
YOU TRY ANY OF THAT "STUFF" YOU TRIED ON US BEFORE, AND WE HAVE ORDERS TO TAKE YOU OUT.
IF YOU EVER WANT TO SEE YOUR MOMMY AGAIN, OR YOUR SISTER...
GET IN THE CAR!!
LET'S GO.
THE POLICE WILL BE HERE SOON.
THEY'LL TAKE YOU AWAY FROM YOUR MOMMY... WHEN THEY FIND OUT WHAT YOU ARE.

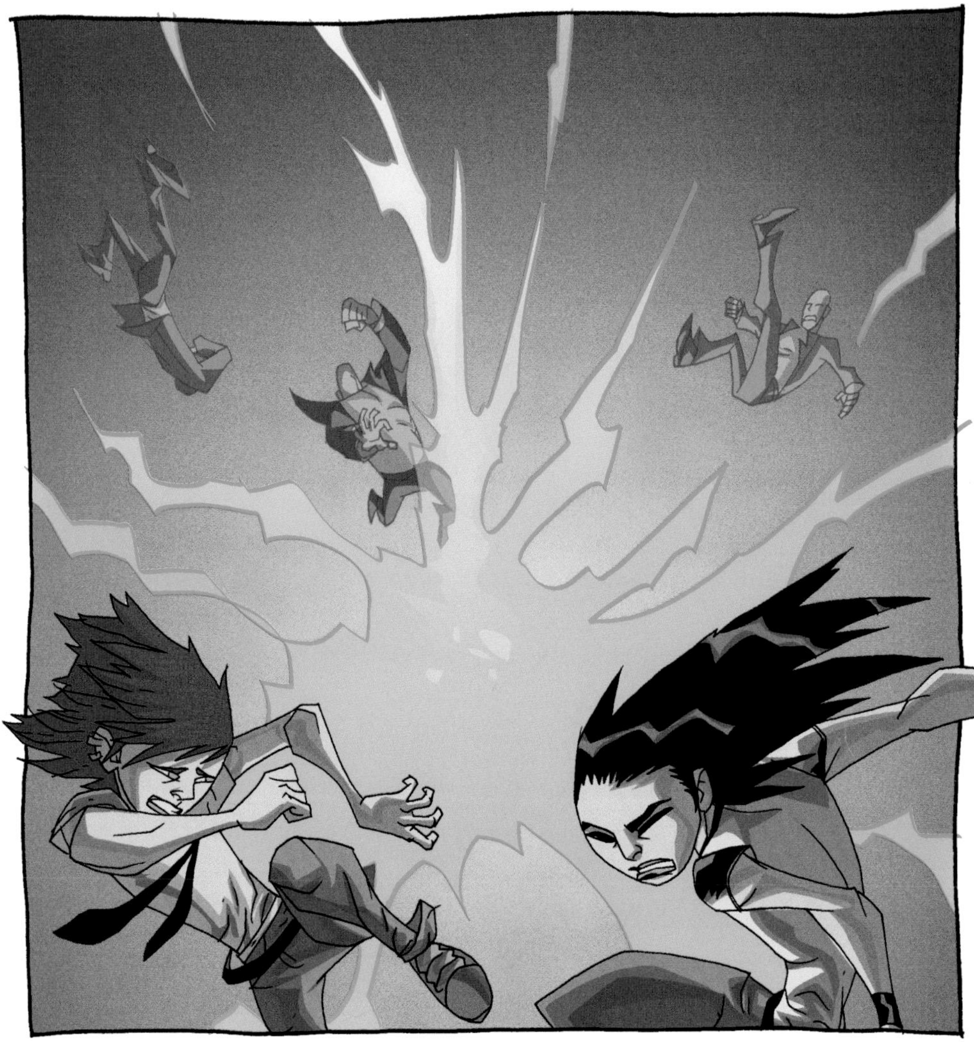

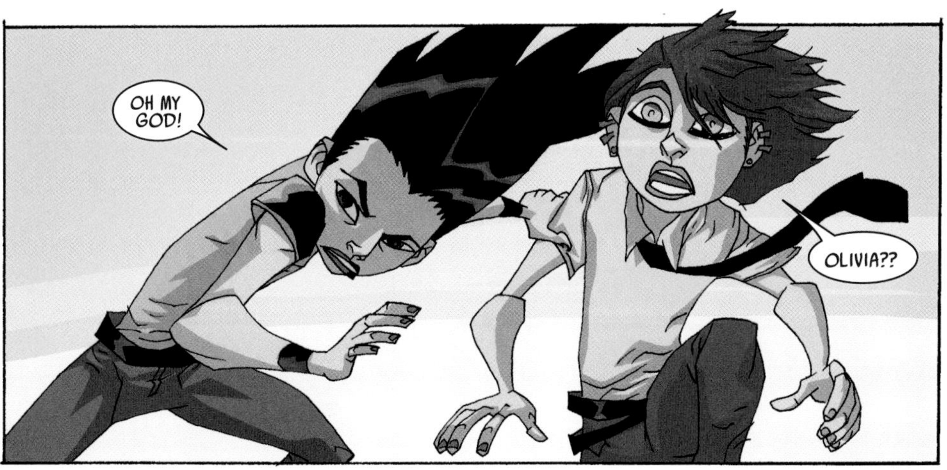
OH MY GOD!
OLIVIA??

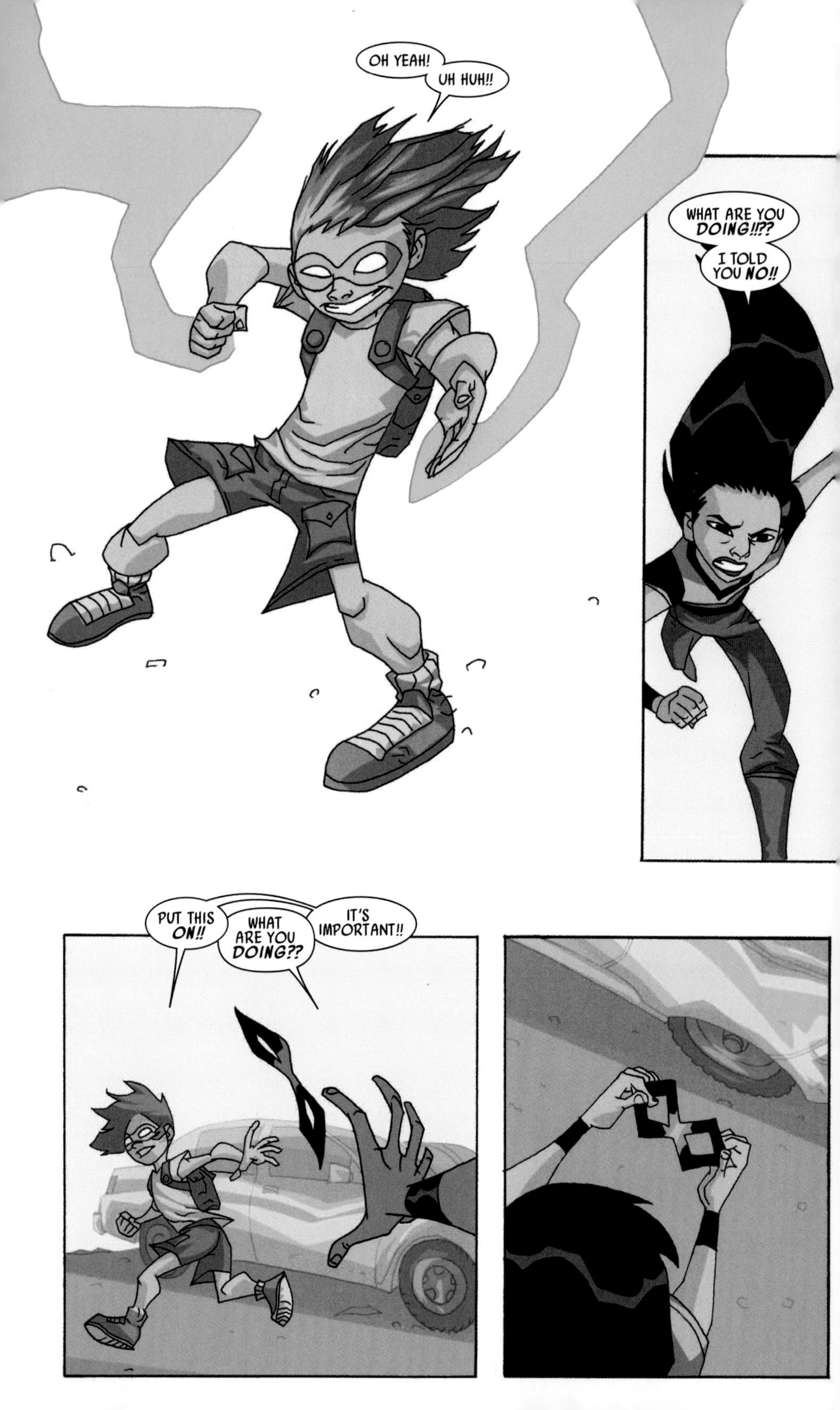
OH YEAH!
UH HUH!!
WHAT ARE YOU DOING!!??
I TOLD YOU NO!!
PUT THIS ON!!
WHAT ARE YOU DOING??
IT'S IMPORTANT!!

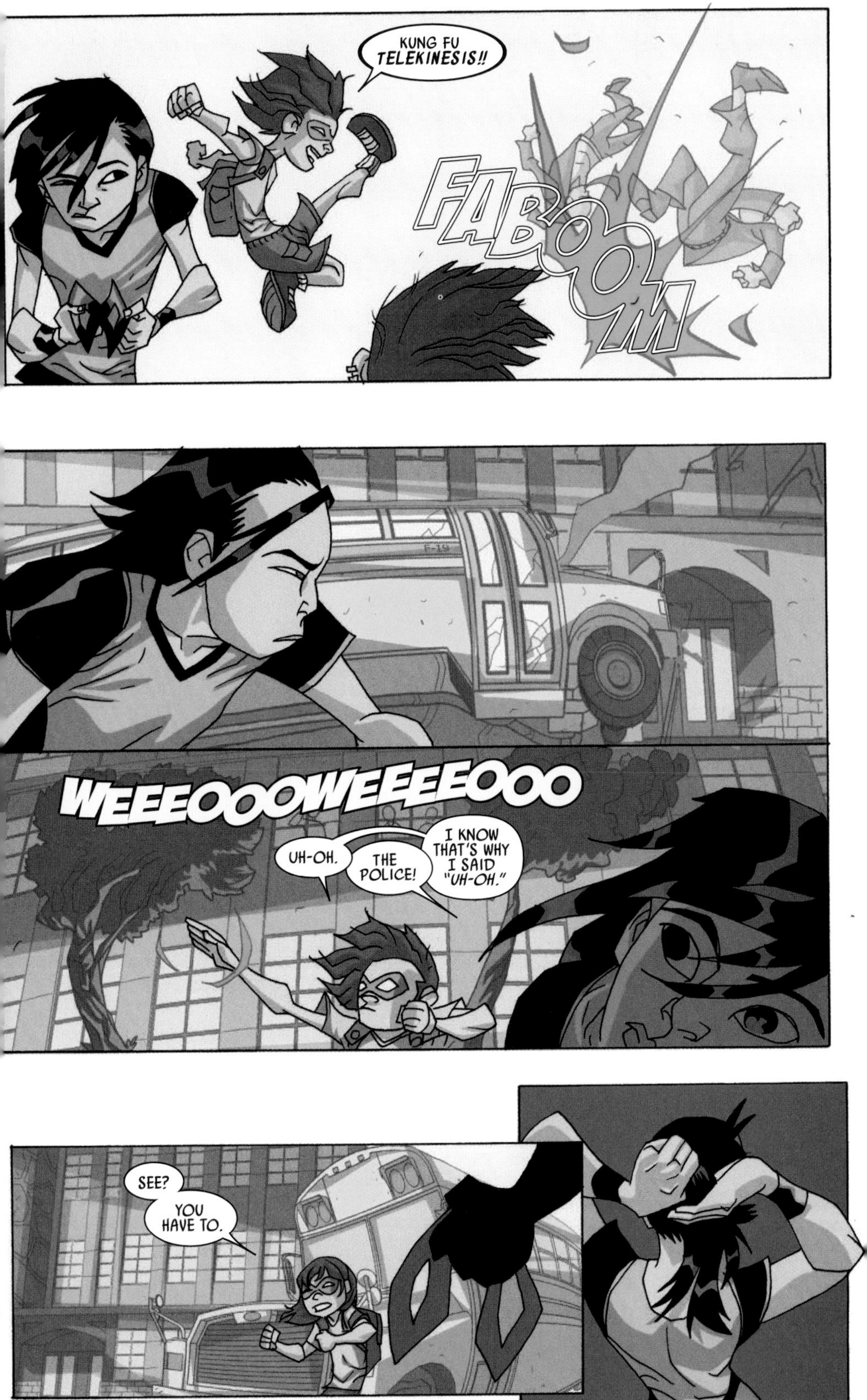
KUNG FU TELEKINESIS!!
FABOOM
WEEEOOOWEEEEOOO
UH-OH.
THE POLICE!
I KNOW THAT'S WHY I SAID "UH-OH."
SEE?
YOU HAVE TO.

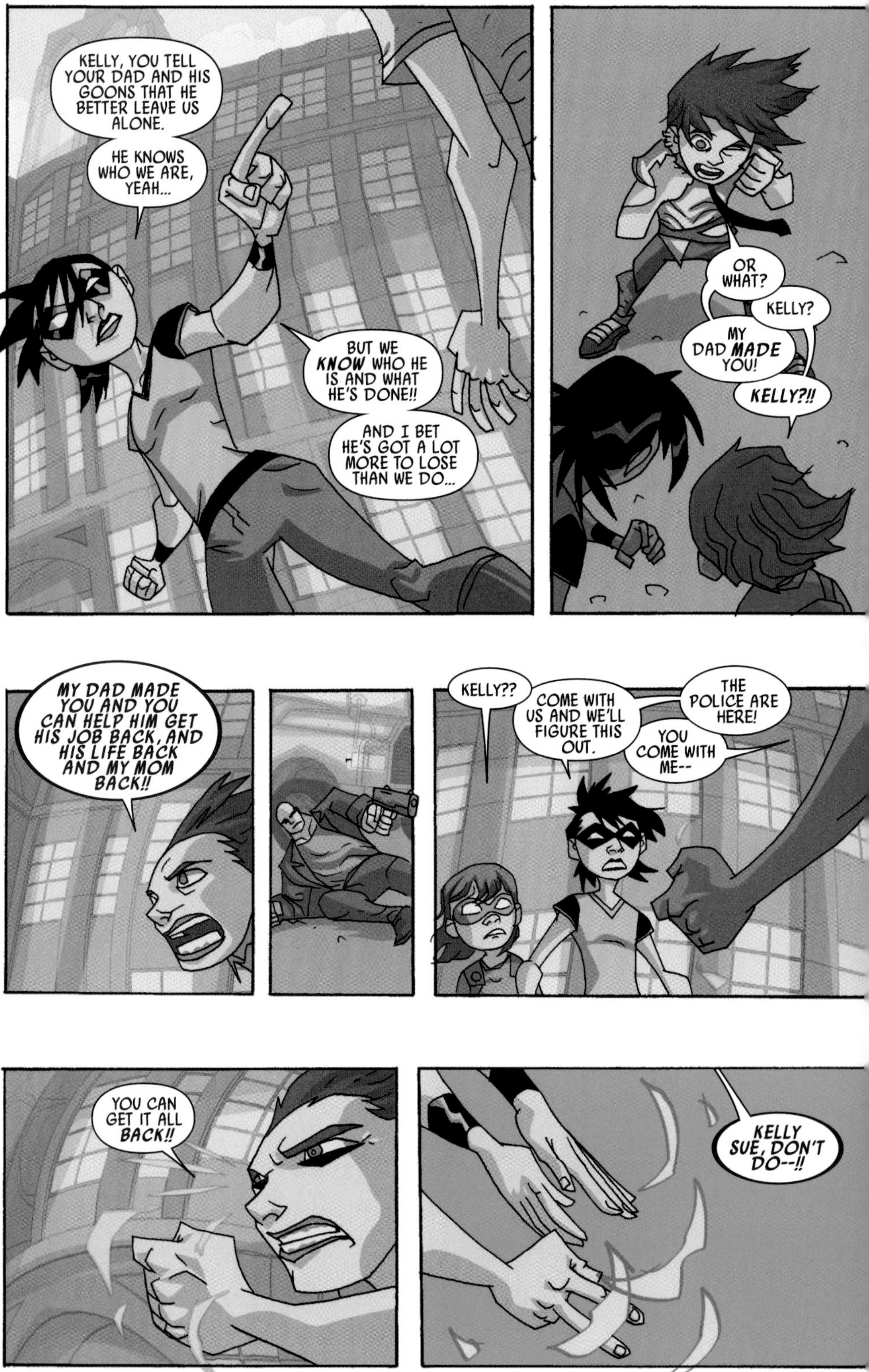
KELLY, YOU TELL YOUR DAD AND HIS GOONS THAT HE BETTER LEAVE US ALONE.
HE KNOWS WHO WE ARE, YEAH...
BUT WE KNOW WHO HE IS AND WHAT HE'S DONE!!
AND I BET HE'S GOT A LOT MORE TO LOSE THAN WE DO...
OR WHAT?
KELLY?
MY DAD MADE YOU!
KELLY?!!
MY DAD MADE YOU AND YOU CAN HELP HIM GET HIS JOB BACK, AND HIS LIFE BACK AND MY MOM BACK!!
KELLY??
COME WITH US AND WE'LL FIGURE THIS OUT.
THE POLICE ARE HERE!
YOU COME WITH ME--
YOU CAN GET IT ALL BACK!!
KELLY SUE, DON'T DO--!!

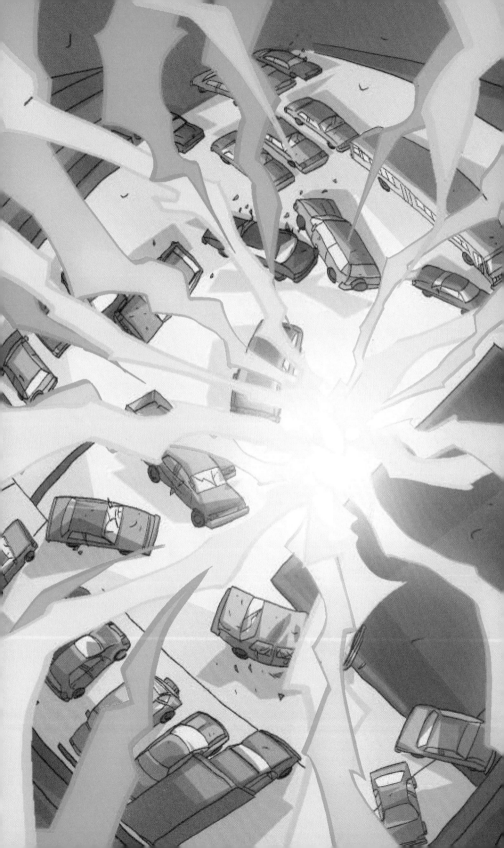

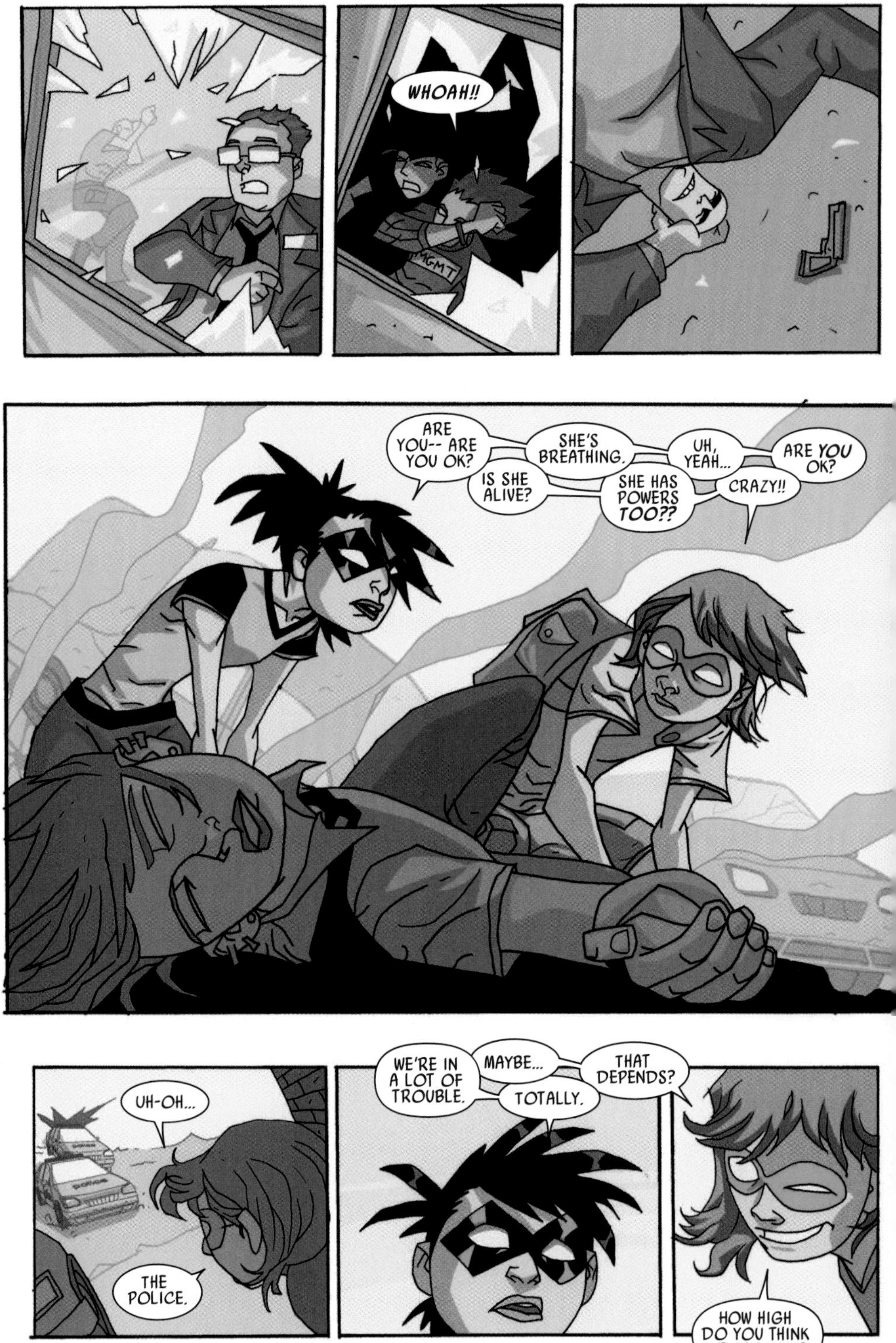
WHOAH!!
ARE YOU-- ARE YOU OK?
IS SHE ALIVE?
SHE'S BREATHING.
SHE HAS POWERS TOO??
UH, YEAH...
CRAZY!!
ARE YOU OK?
UH-OH...
THE POLICE.
WE'RE IN A LOT OF TROUBLE.
MAYBE...
TOTALLY.
THAT DEPENDS?
HOW HIGH DO YOU THINK WE CAN JUMP?

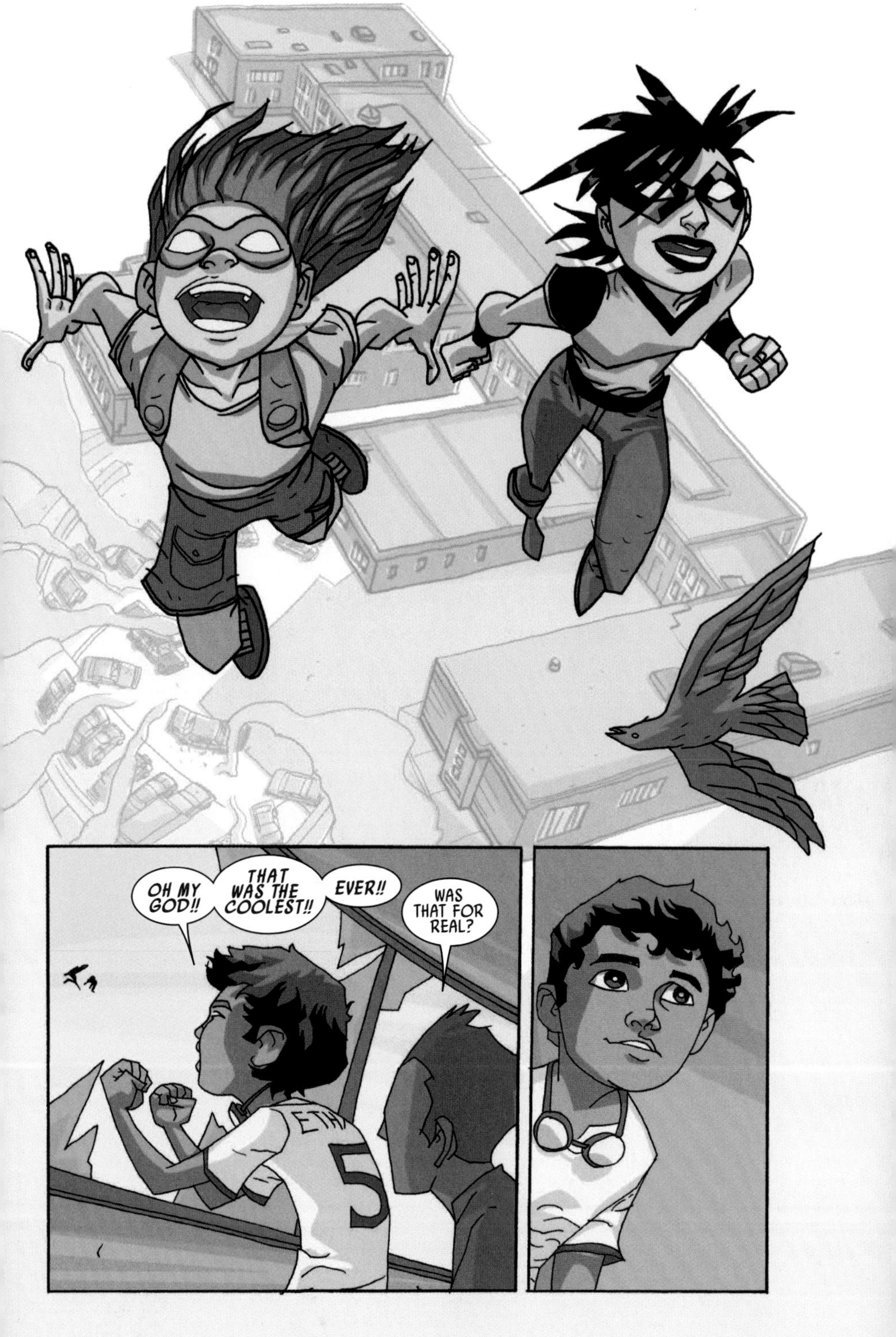
OH MY GOD!!
THAT WAS THE COOLEST!!
EVER!!
WAS THAT FOR REAL?
ETH
5

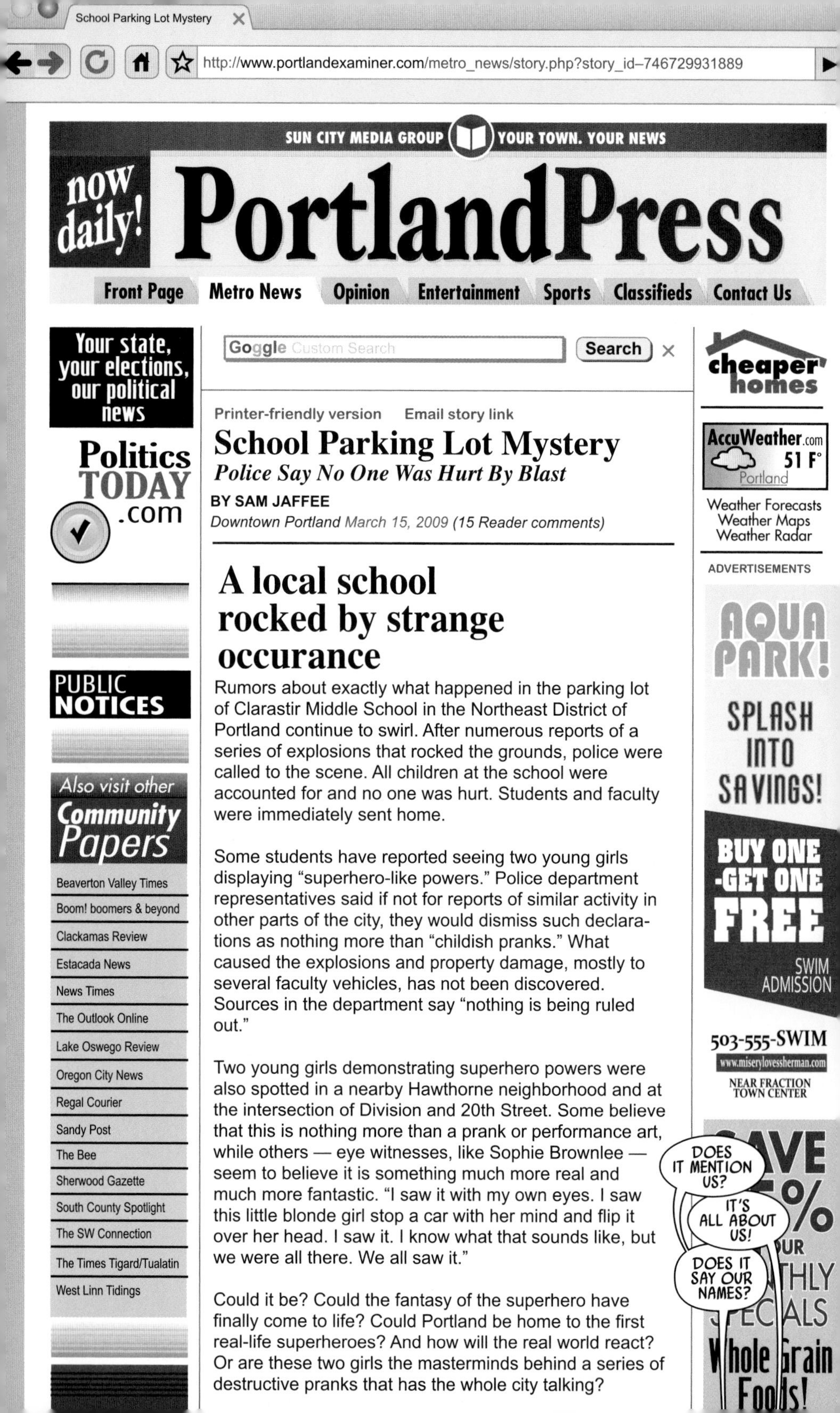

School Parking Lot Mystery

http://www.portlandexaminer.com/metro_news/story.php?story_id–746729931889

now daily! PortlandPress

School Parking Lot Mystery

Police Say No One Was Hurt By Blast

BY SAM JAFFEE

Downtown Portland March 15, 2009 (15 Reader comments)

A local school rocked by strange occurance

Rumors about exactly what happened in the parking lot of Clarastir Middle School in the Northeast District of Portland continue to swirl. After numerous reports of a series of explosions that rocked the grounds, police were called to the scene. All children at the school were accounted for and no one was hurt. Students and faculty were immediately sent home.

Some students have reported seeing two young girls displaying "superhero-like powers." Police department representatives said if not for reports of similar activity in other parts of the city, they would dismiss such declarations as nothing more than "childish pranks." What caused the explosions and property damage, mostly to several faculty vehicles, has not been discovered. Sources in the department say "nothing is being ruled out."

Two young girls demonstrating superhero powers were also spotted in a nearby Hawthorne neighborhood and at the intersection of Division and 20th Street. Some believe that this is nothing more than a prank or performance art, while others — eye witnesses, like Sophie Brownlee — seem to believe it is something much more real and much more fantastic. "I saw it with my own eyes. I saw this little blonde girl stop a car with her mind and flip it over her head. I saw it. I know what that sounds like, but we were all there. We all saw it."

Could it be? Could the fantasy of the superhero have finally come to life? Could Portland be home to the first real-life superheroes? And how will the real world react? Or are these two girls the masterminds behind a series of destructive pranks that has the whole city talking?

DOES IT MENTION US?
IT'S ALL ABOUT US!
DOES IT SAY OUR NAMES?

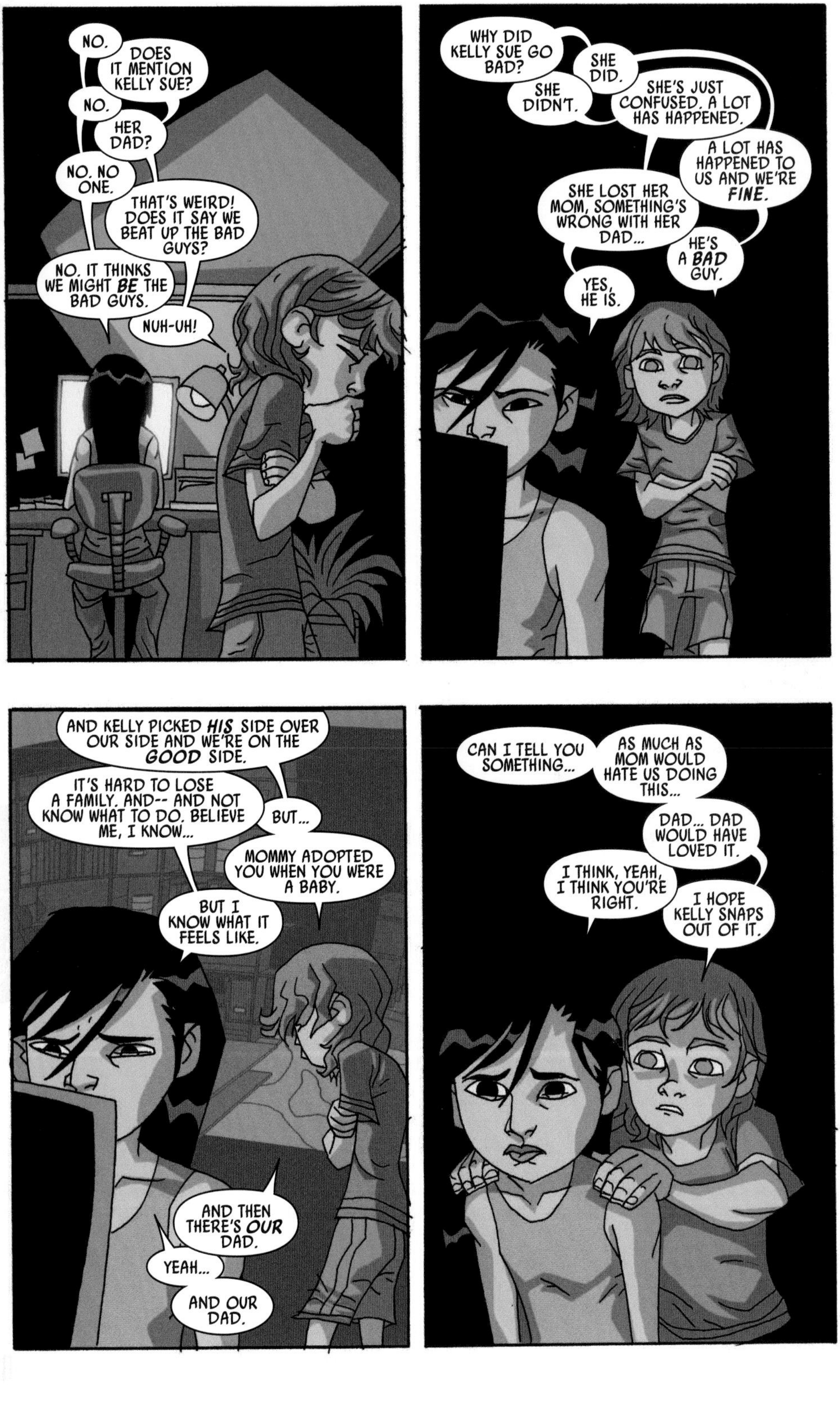
NO.
DOES IT MENTION KELLY SUE?
NO.
HER DAD?
NO. NO ONE.
THAT'S WEIRD! DOES IT SAY WE BEAT UP THE BAD GUYS?
NO. IT THINKS WE MIGHT *BE* THE BAD GUYS.
NUH-UH!
WHY DID KELLY SUE GO BAD?
SHE DIDN'T.
SHE DID.
SHE'S JUST CONFUSED. A LOT HAS HAPPENED.
A LOT HAS HAPPENED TO US AND WE'RE *FINE*.
SHE LOST HER MOM, SOMETHING'S WRONG WITH HER DAD...
HE'S A *BAD* GUY.
YES, HE IS.
AND KELLY PICKED *HIS* SIDE OVER OUR SIDE AND WE'RE ON THE *GOOD* SIDE.
IT'S HARD TO LOSE A FAMILY. AND-- AND NOT KNOW WHAT TO DO. BELIEVE ME, I KNOW...
BUT...
MOMMY ADOPTED YOU WHEN YOU WERE A BABY.
BUT I KNOW WHAT IT FEELS LIKE.
AND THEN THERE'S *OUR* DAD.
YEAH...
AND OUR DAD.
CAN I TELL YOU SOMETHING...
AS MUCH AS MOM WOULD HATE US DOING THIS...
DAD... DAD WOULD HAVE LOVED IT.
I THINK, YEAH, I THINK YOU'RE RIGHT.
I HOPE KELLY SNAPS OUT OF IT.

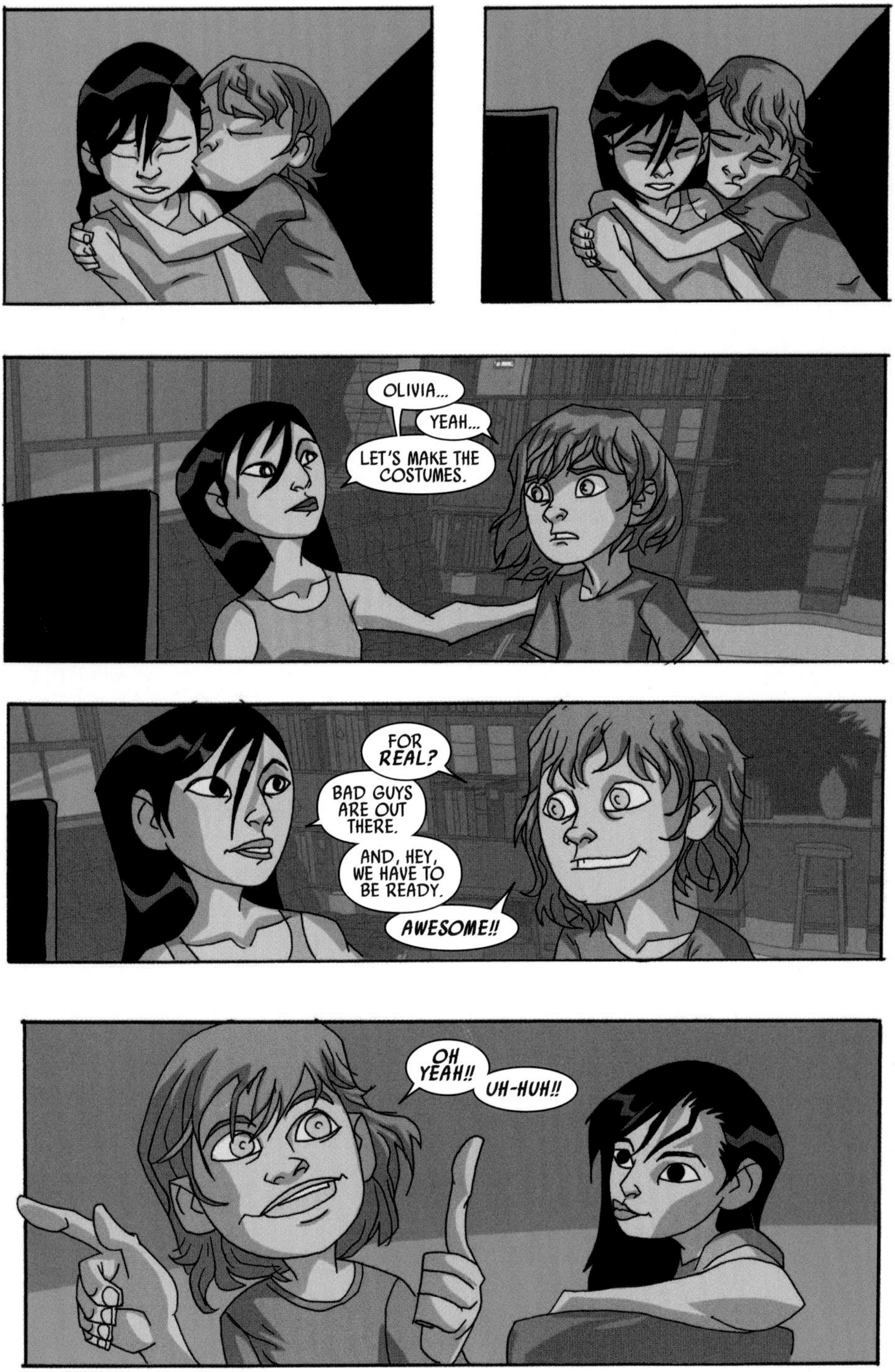

OLIVIA...
YEAH...
LET'S MAKE THE COSTUMES.
FOR REAL?
BAD GUYS ARE OUT THERE.
AND, HEY, WE HAVE TO BE READY.
AWESOME!!
OH YEAH!!
UH-HUH!!

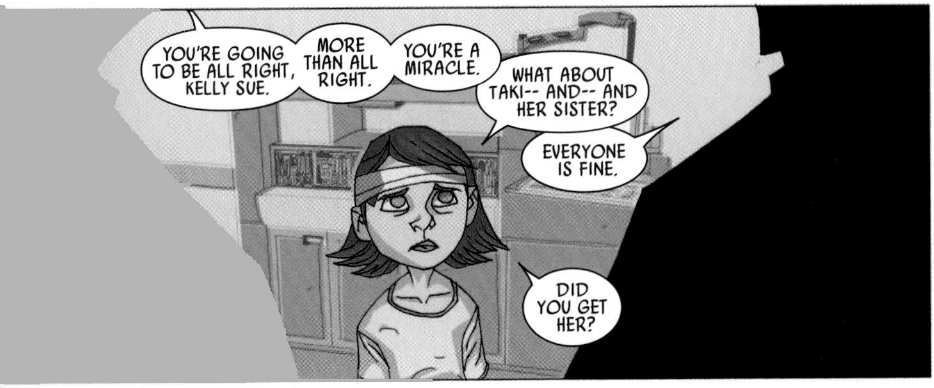
YOU'RE GOING TO BE ALL RIGHT, KELLY SUE.
MORE THAN ALL RIGHT.
YOU'RE A MIRACLE.
WHAT ABOUT TAKI-- AND-- AND HER SISTER?
EVERYONE IS FINE.
DID YOU GET HER?

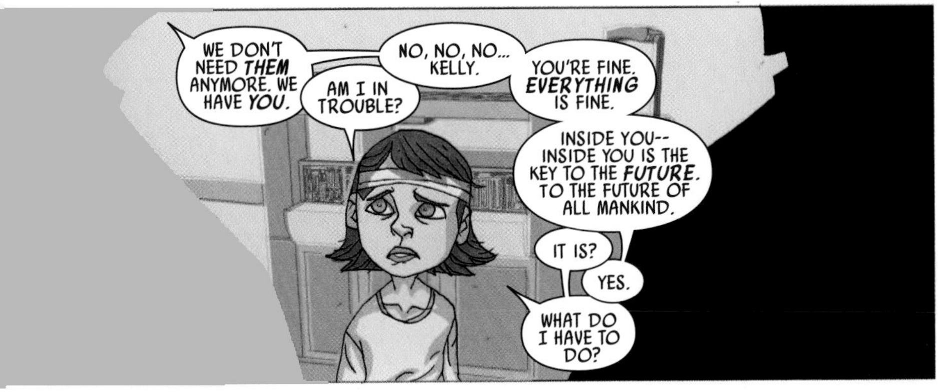
WE DON'T NEED ***THEM*** ANYMORE. WE HAVE ***YOU***.
AM I IN TROUBLE?
NO, NO, NO... KELLY.
YOU'RE FINE. ***EVERYTHING*** IS FINE.
INSIDE YOU-- INSIDE YOU IS THE KEY TO THE ***FUTURE***. TO THE FUTURE OF ALL MANKIND.
IT IS?
YES.
WHAT DO I HAVE TO DO?

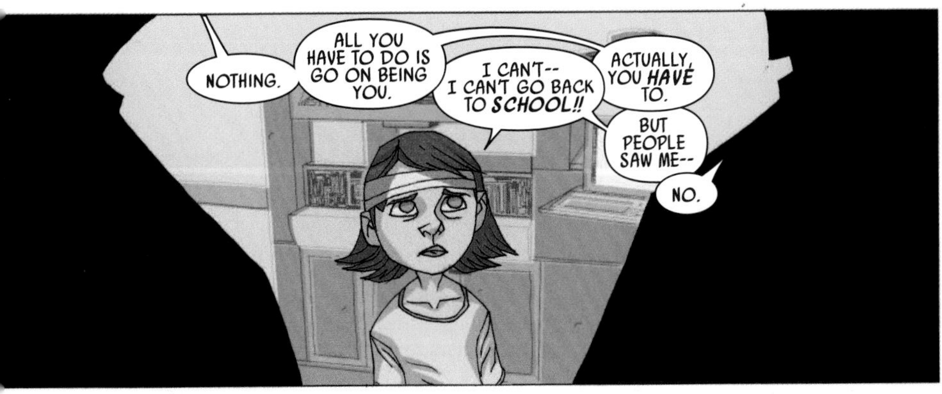
NOTHING.
ALL YOU HAVE TO DO IS GO ON BEING YOU.
I CAN'T-- I CAN'T GO BACK TO ***SCHOOL!!***
ACTUALLY, YOU ***HAVE*** TO.
BUT PEOPLE SAW ME--
NO.

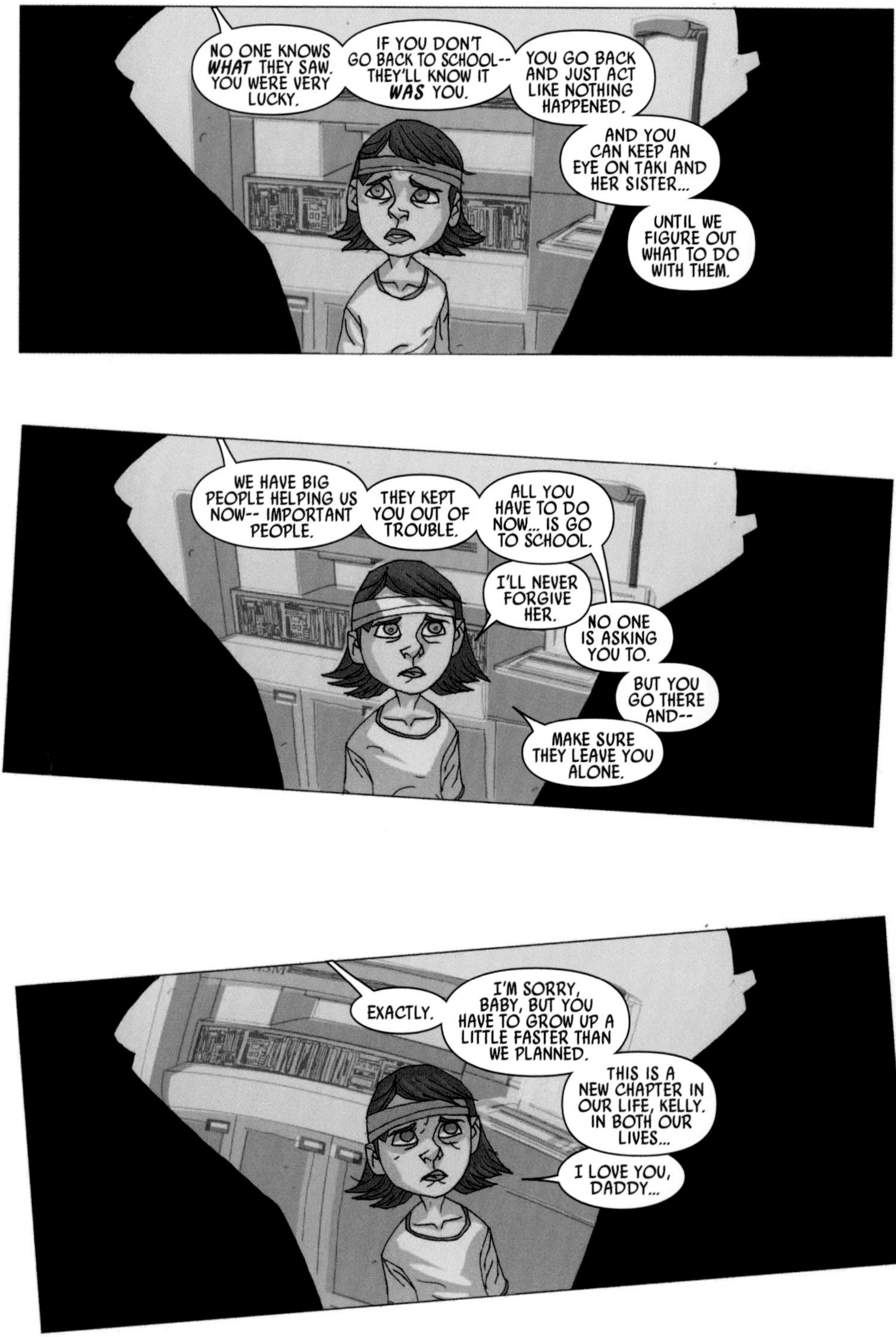
NO ONE KNOWS *WHAT* THEY SAW. YOU WERE VERY LUCKY.
IF YOU DON'T GO BACK TO SCHOOL-- THEY'LL KNOW IT *WAS* YOU.
YOU GO BACK AND JUST ACT LIKE NOTHING HAPPENED.
AND YOU CAN KEEP AN EYE ON TAKI AND HER SISTER...
UNTIL WE FIGURE OUT WHAT TO DO WITH THEM.
WE HAVE BIG PEOPLE HELPING US NOW-- IMPORTANT PEOPLE.
THEY KEPT YOU OUT OF TROUBLE.
ALL YOU HAVE TO DO NOW... IS GO TO SCHOOL.
I'LL NEVER FORGIVE HER.
NO ONE IS ASKING YOU TO.
BUT YOU GO THERE AND--
MAKE SURE THEY LEAVE YOU ALONE.
EXACTLY.
I'M SORRY, BABY, BUT YOU HAVE TO GROW UP A LITTLE FASTER THAN WE PLANNED.
THIS IS A NEW CHAPTER IN OUR LIFE, KELLY. IN BOTH OUR LIVES...
I LOVE YOU, DADDY...

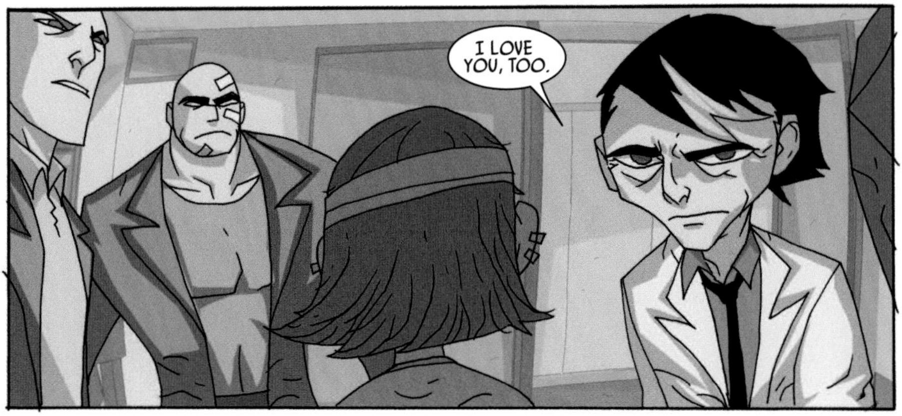
I LOVE YOU, TOO.

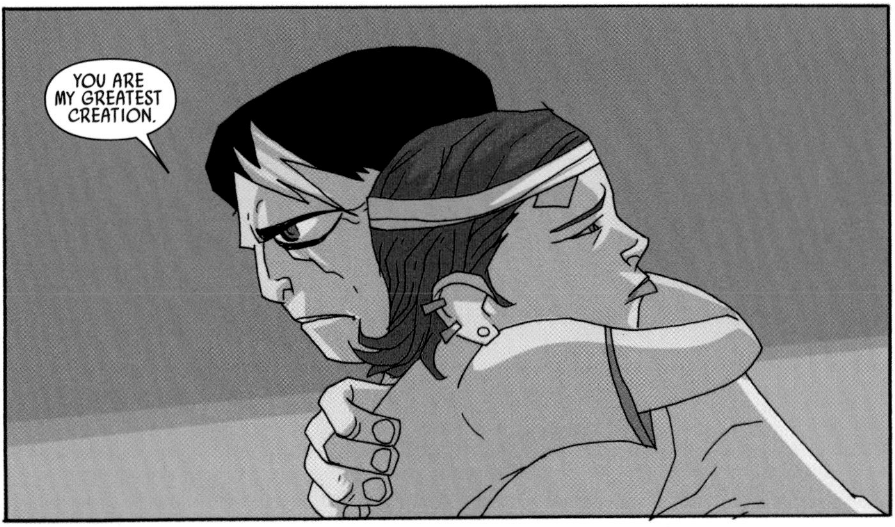
YOU ARE MY GREATEST CREATION.

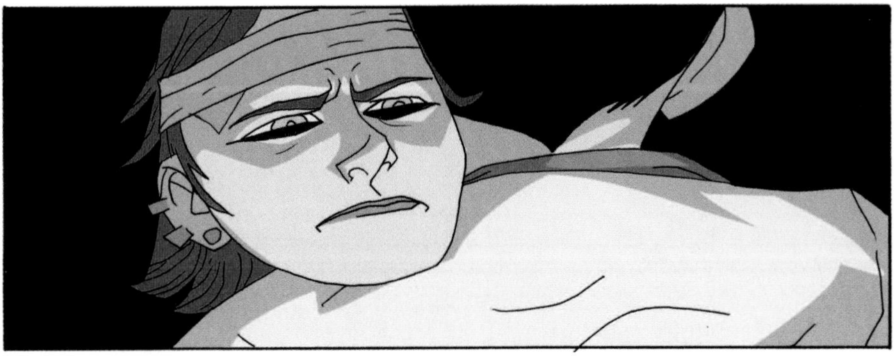

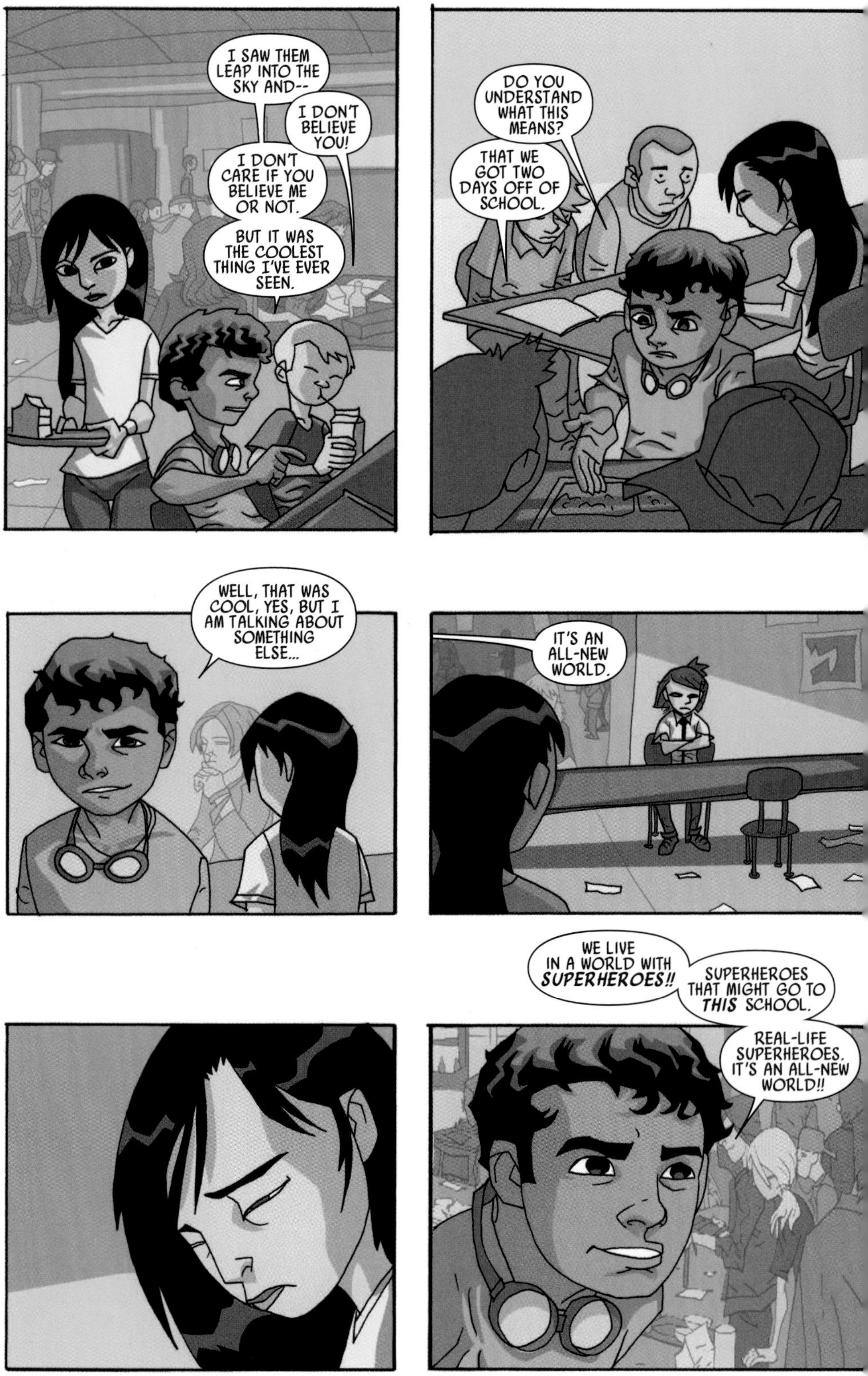
I SAW THEM LEAP INTO THE SKY AND--
I DON'T BELIEVE YOU!
I DON'T CARE IF YOU BELIEVE ME OR NOT.
BUT IT WAS THE COOLEST THING I'VE EVER SEEN.
DO YOU UNDERSTAND WHAT THIS MEANS?
THAT WE GOT TWO DAYS OFF OF SCHOOL.
WELL, THAT WAS COOL, YES, BUT I AM TALKING ABOUT SOMETHING ELSE...
IT'S AN ALL-NEW WORLD.
WE LIVE IN A WORLD WITH SUPERHEROES!!
SUPERHEROES THAT MIGHT GO TO THIS SCHOOL.
REAL-LIFE SUPERHEROES. IT'S AN ALL-NEW WORLD!!

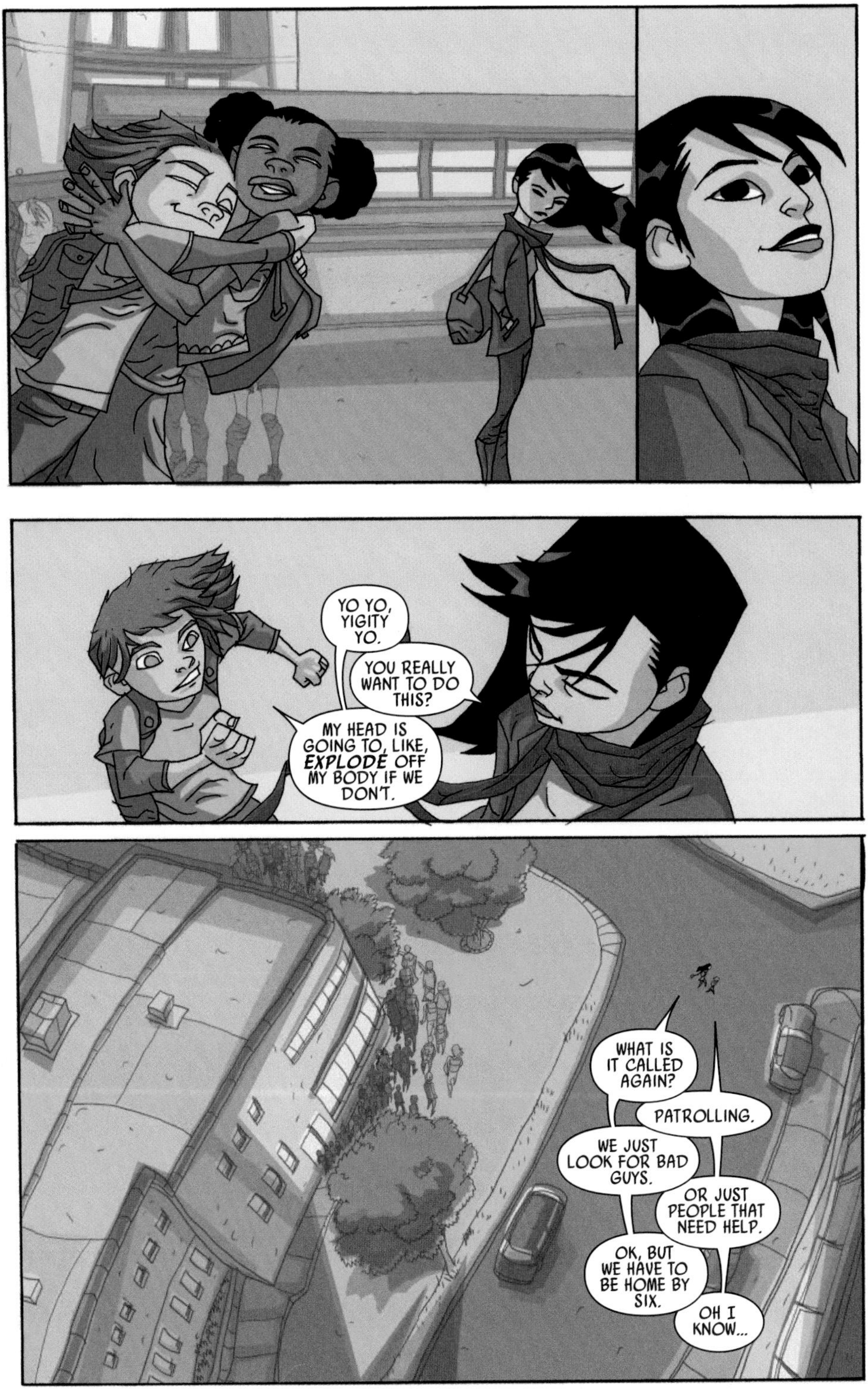
YO YO, YIGITY YO.
YOU REALLY WANT TO DO THIS?
MY HEAD IS GOING TO, LIKE, **EXPLODE** OFF MY BODY IF WE DON'T.
WHAT IS IT CALLED AGAIN?
PATROLLING.
WE JUST LOOK FOR BAD GUYS.
OR JUST PEOPLE THAT NEED HELP.
OK, BUT WE HAVE TO BE HOME BY SIX.
OH I KNOW...

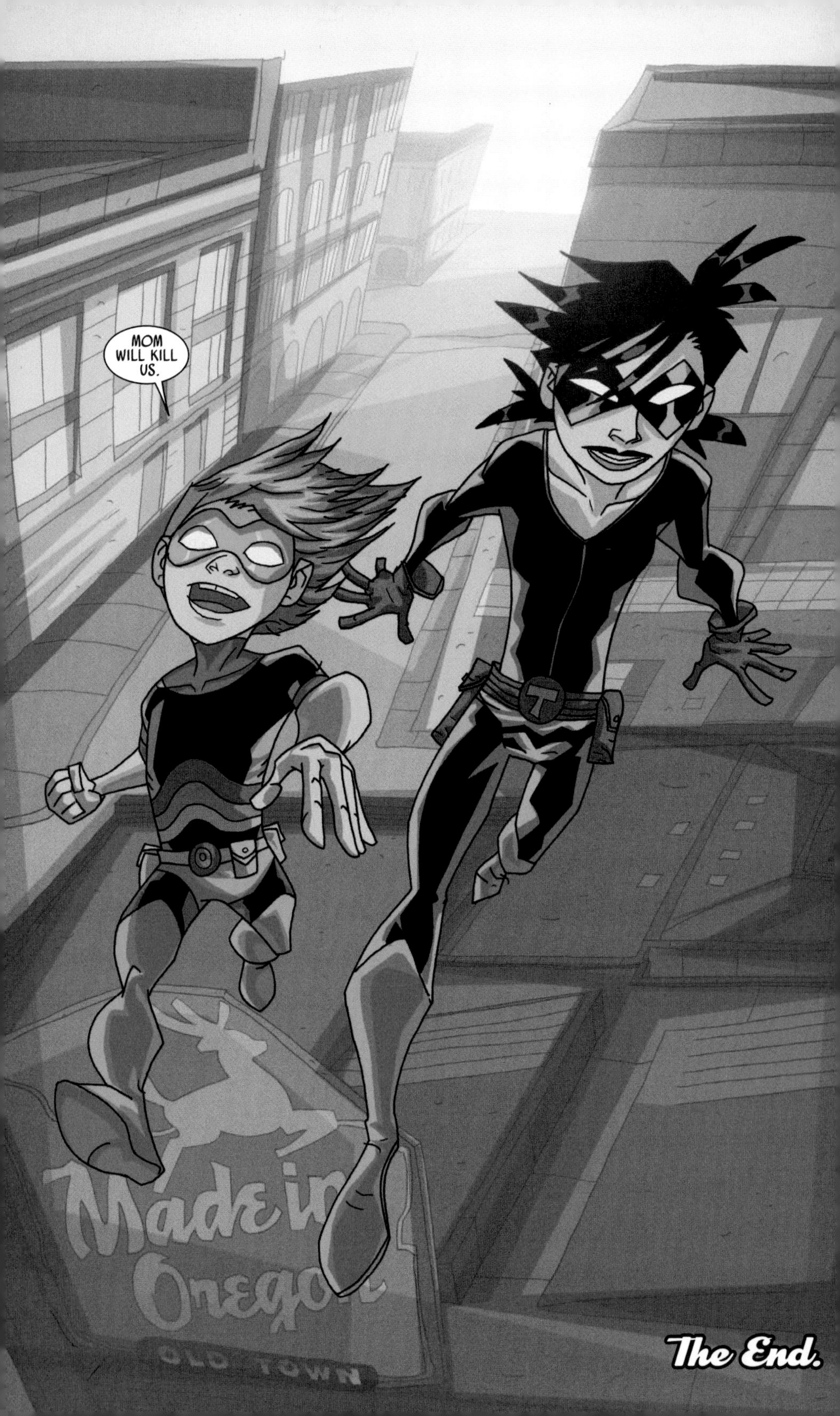
MOM WILL KILL US.
Made in Oregon
OLD TOWN
The End.

MIKE OEMING SKETCHBOOK

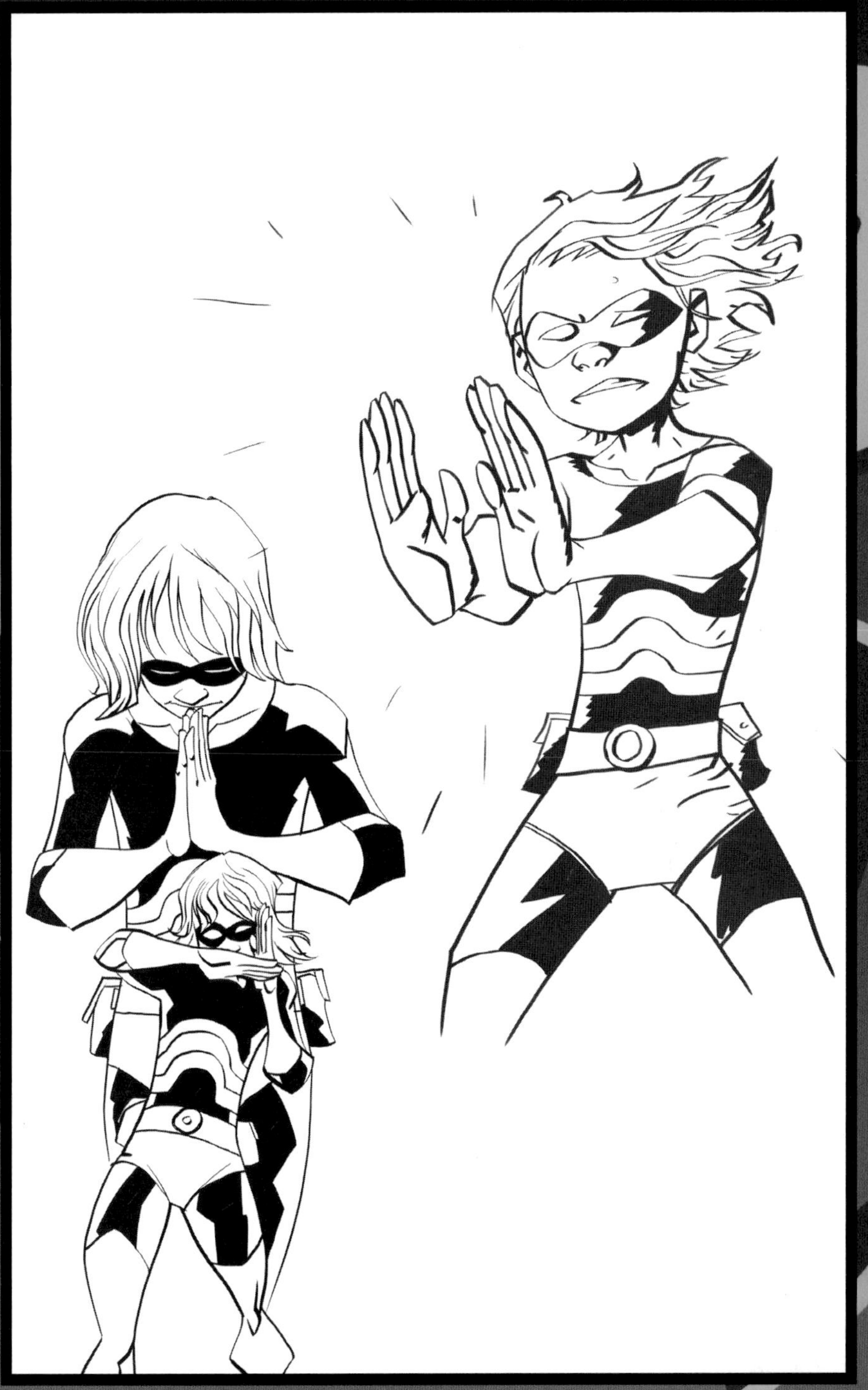

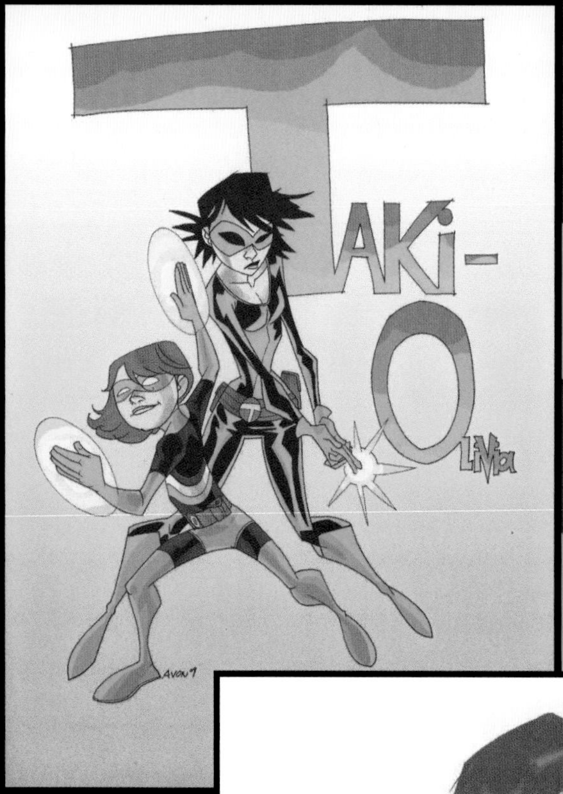
TAKi-
OLiVia

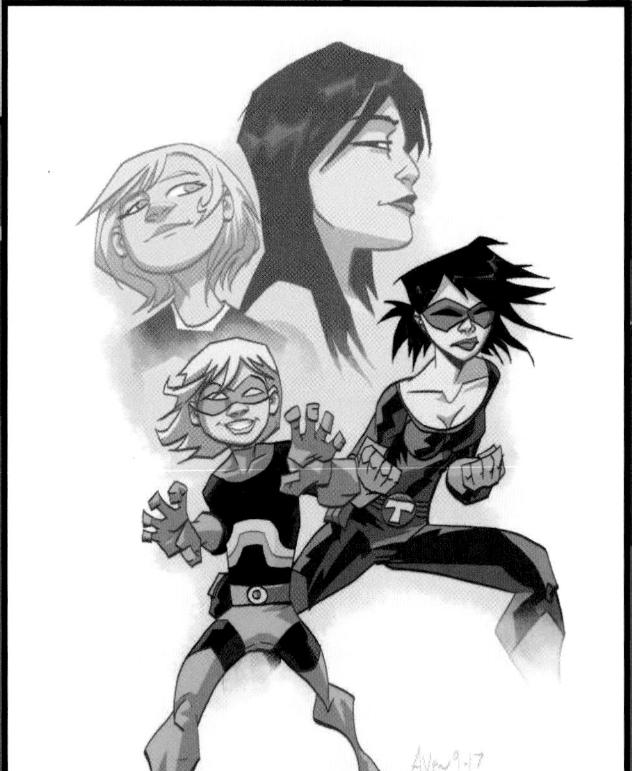

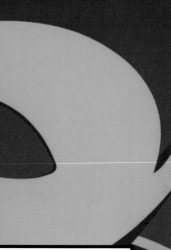

COLORS BY VAL STAPLES